Ryan + Sophia,
Be Blessed always!
Aunt Angie
2/10/16

Hidden Treasures REVEALED

Truths that will transform your life!

ANGIE BUHRKE

Hidden Treasures Revealed

ISBN # 978-0-692-52562-3

Editor: Renee Gray-Wilburn

Cover design & layout: Satoshi Yamamoto

Printed in the United States of America.

Table of Contents

Acknowledgments

I want to thank my Lord and Savior, Jesus Christ, for another opportunity to share what He has taught me over the years. I am truly grateful for His faithfulness toward me.

A special thank-you to my husband, Al, who demonstrates more than anyone else I know, the true, unconditional love of God—not only to others, but to me personally.

I'd also like to thank Renee Gray-Wilburn for her awesome ability to make it sound "just right" on paper. She has the gift of "changing everything without changing anything."

And thank you, Andrew Wommack, for sharing your life-changing revelation with us.

Introduction

Yea, if thou criest after knowledge, and liftest up thy voice for understanding; If thou seekest her as silver, and searchest for her as for hid treasures; Then shalt thou understand the fear of the LORD, and find the knowledge of God.

Proverbs 2:3-5

Thinking back to my childhood days I remember playing a game called "Hide-and-Seek." It was a fun, exciting game that we could play anywhere at anytime. It seems to have remained a very popular game among children as well as some adults to this day. Various versions of the game, which include "Hide-and-Seek" in the dark, are also quite popular, although a bit more challenging.

The game is simple. The seeker counts to ten, or whatever number he or she chooses, giving the others a chance to find a hiding place. Then the seeker declares with a loud voice: "Ready or not, here I come!" and the hunt is on. The search is with much focus, as if searching for treasure, and if the seeker searches diligently and does not give up, he or she eventually finds those who are hiding.

The Bible is full of treasures—precious, highly valued truths that enable us to live life victoriously. According to the above scripture, if we seek knowledge and understanding like we would silver or hidden treasures, we will find the wisdom of God. Not only will we receive godly wisdom, but as we search the scriptures we will receive revelation knowledge. Receiving revelation is when we are enlightened in a certain area. We can read the same passage over and over again for years, but then suddenly we have that "wow" moment when something is revealed that cements a certain truth for us.

There are two types of people in this world: believers and nonbelievers. Unless a person is born again, he or she will never receive revelation of God's Word: *But if our gospel be hid, it is hid to them that are lost* (2 Cor. 4:3).

But even if someone *is* born again, it is still possible for that person to never receive revelation knowledge. Why?

There are a few reasons.

First, some are not seeking. It takes time and effort to study the scriptures.

And ye shall seek me, and find me, when ye shall search for me with all your heart. Jeremiah 29:13

Revelation comes by reading the Word and living that Word in our daily life; if we don't put the work into it, we won't receive it. We have to have a "ready or not, here I come" attitude and then search the scriptures. The title of this book is *Hidden Treasures,* but the treasures in God's Word are not hidden *from* the believer; they are hidden *for* the believer. It just takes some digging to find them.

I remember when I worked as a teenager I paid my parents room and board weekly. At the end of my senior year in high school, I had an opportunity to travel to Italy with my classmates. I began saving my money earlier that year. Shortly before my trip my mother handed me an envelope. It was filled with all the room and board money I paid her over that past year. What a blessing to me! She was hiding the money *for* me, not *from* me.

It's the same with God. His Word is powerful and, if applied in our lives, will allow us to live the abundant life Jesus already died to give us. He wants to reveal His truths to us in such a way that it will benefit us in this life while glorifying God at the same time. These truths are kept *for* us and will only be revealed to those who want to find them.

I always wondered why, after Jesus ascended into heaven, those in the Upper Room had to wait ten days for the promised Holy Spirit to come. Acts chapter 1 tells us that there were about 120 people in the Upper Room. There were probably more people outside. I believe during those ten days those who were just not that interested probably left; they may have thought it wasn't worth the wait, or maybe some just gave up because of unbelief creeping in as the days progressed. I believe the Holy Spirit waited until only those who were truly serious about Him remained. These are the seekers who will find God every time.

The second reason some do not receive revelation is because they do not have ears to hear. We are not talking about physical hearing, but spiritual hearing. Born-again believers have ears to hear. *But ye have an unction from the Holy One, and ye know all things (1 John 2:20).* The

Holy Spirit quickens us so that we can understand spiritual things; thus, having ears to hear.

But we make the choice if we want to hear or not. Jesus said in Mark 4:9, *He that hath ears to hear, let him hear*. Our hearing is blocked because our heart has become hardened to the things of God. Wherever our attention is focused is where our heart becomes softened; wherever our attention is not focused is where our heart becomes hardened. If our attention is toward God's Word, then our hearts will be softened so our ears can actually hear what the Spirit longs to teach us.

The third reason Christians don't get revelation is because they are wise in their own eyes.

> *At that time Jesus answered and said, I thank thee, O Father, Lord of heaven and earth, because thou hast hid these things from the wise and prudent, and hast revealed them unto babes. Even so, Father: for so it seemed good in thy sight. Matthew 11:25-26*

Again, it's not that God hides these truths from us; He reserves them for us, and we can have them whenever we decide to seek them. But it's difficult for those to receive who believe that they know everything there is to know about God yet, in reality, they only have a head knowledge of Him.

Some people are just too smart for God. I've seen people who have struggled to understand the truths of God's Word because they are using their heads—the same heads that got them their Master's degree. I'm not against education, but this is a heart issue, not a head issue. Knowing God is to experience Him and His love for us in our everyday life. Our head could never in a lifetime grasp what one heart can experience in just one moment with God.

God's truths are revealed to the "babes." The original Greek meaning of this word is "a little child, a minor, unskilled, untaught; an immature Christian." When I first became born again I knew nothing but that God loved and accepted me. I was so excited that it caused me to seek the treasures in His Word and look to the scriptures to change me daily. I may not have been the sharpest knife in the drawer, but I managed to receive *my* Master's degree also—my Master being Jesus Christ, my Lord and Savior. I was changed forever. And I continue to let the Word reveal truths to me to help me live victoriously every day of my life.

This is what this book is all about. It's a compilation of various topics the Lord has taught me over the years. I am blessed and excited to share them with you, and my prayer is that these lessons will encourage you to dig deeper for yourself and reap the benefits of seeing victory in every area of your life!

Chapter One

As He Is

Herein is our love made perfect, that we may have boldness in the day of judgment: because as he is, so are we in this world.

1 John 4:17

Years ago a friend told me that she felt it was time to "find herself." She said she needed to find her identity, explaining that things were slowing down in her life, which would give her time to do just that. Another woman told me that she didn't even know who she was anymore and that she has never really focused on herself. Now was the time for her and her alone; she wanted to give herself 100 percent attention. She felt she gave and gave to others over the years, but now it was time for her. Others have said to me that since their children were now grown they would have time to discover themselves. They began by researching their family tree. All of these women are Christians.

There are also many men and women who say they are going through a mid-life crisis with some of these same issues. I realize that many people feel this way. They have been busy all their lives working and raising children, and it seemed they never had any time for themselves. There comes a time in their lives when they begin to sense an emptiness inside that needs to be filled with something. They figure that if they can find out **who** they really are, it would solve their problem. It would seem they became so wrapped up in their daily routines and busyness of life that they identified themselves by what they were most involved in. My husband and I both understand the busyness of working and raising a family; it can get hectic and overwhelming at times. I am not minimizing the work involved in taking care of a family or having a career.

It's not that people get lost over the years and then have to find themselves. I believe there was always emptiness inside of them, but dealing with it was put off because they were so busy with other things. Either the problem was a lack of understanding as to **who** God says they are, or they in fact *did* understand but did not cultivate that knowledge.

Asking "Who am I?" is not the real question people are asking. After all, people have names; they have addresses; they have families; they have social security numbers! I think what people are asking instead is "Why am I here? Is there even a purpose for my being here? Is this all there is to life?"

There was a time in my life when I, too, was confused as to the reason for life. I was a Christian and understood some things, but until I found out **who** I really became once I was born again, life was full of questions. I wanted to be a "good" Christian, but it seemed an impossibility at that time; I was always falling short. But all my questions were answered when I received the revelation of who I *really* am. From that point on, my whole life was built on that foundational truth.

Let's look at three scriptures regarding being baptized in Christ:

> *Buried with him in baptism, wherein also ye are risen with him through the faith of the operation of God, who hath raised him from the dead. Colossians 2:12*

> *For as many of you as have been baptized into Christ have put on Christ. Galatians 3:27*

Know ye not, that so many of us as were baptized into Jesus Christ were baptized into his death? Therefore we are buried with him by baptism into death: that like as Christ was raised up from the dead by the glory of the Father, even so we also should walk in newness of life. Romans 6:3-4

These scriptures are not referring to water baptism but rather being born again. Being baptized into Christ means taking on a brand-new permanent identity—changing from "in Adam" to "in Christ." We are not the same people once we are baptized into Christ. Our spirit man changes to "in Christ."

Second Corinthians 5:17 describes what happens when we become born again:

Therefore if any man be in Christ, he is a new creature: old things are passed away; behold, all things are become new.

A whole new nature has been given to us; the nature of Christ Himself. We became NEW and received our new identity!

Also, 2 Corinthians 5:21 tells us what else happens…

For he hath made him to be sin for us, who knew no sin; that we might be made the righteousness of God in him.

The word *righteousness* simply means "the state of him who is as he ought to be, righteous, the condition acceptable to God." Jesus became my sin and suffered the wrath of God for it. I love how Bible teacher Andrew Wommack says it: "He became what I was so I could become what He was." He was righteous, and so we become righteous. We no longer should call ourselves sinners; we are the righteousness of God. There are no more barriers between God and mankind.

Colossians 2:9-10 tell us what this righteousness includes:

For in him dwelleth all the fullness of the Godhead bodily (v. 9).

Because Jesus had the fullness of His Father inside of Him, so do we! Every bit of who Jesus is resides inside of us. We didn't get just a part of Jesus; we got every part of

Jesus. We didn't get His love but not His peace; we didn't get His knowledge but not His wisdom; we didn't get His healing but not His protection; we got all of Him! He is inside our spirit man.

> *And ye are complete in him, which is the head of all principality and power (v. 10).*

The word *complete* means "fill up to the top, level up, satisfy, supply liberally, cause to abound, full measure, fill to the brim, to render perfect, carry through to the end." So we can then say that we exist in the presence and power of God Himself! Wow! Exactly how much power do we have? Ephesians 1:19-22 tells us.

> *And what is the exceeding greatness of his power to usward who believe, according to the working of his mighty power, which he wrought in Christ, when he raised him from the dead, and set him at his own right hand in the heavenly places, far above all principality, and power, and might, and dominion, and every name that is named, not only in this world, but also in that which is to come: And hath put all things under his feet, and gave him to be the head over all things to the church.*

We have the same power that raised Jesus from the dead. This power is for our benefit. It enables us to overcome all circumstances in life as well as all demonic influences. Jesus is the head of all principality and power, and so are we (see Eph. 1:21). Through His power we can heal the sick, cleanse the lepers, raise the dead, and cast out devils (see Matt. 10:8). Once we understand the power we have, we can overcome any identity problem.

One of my favorite scriptures is 1 John 4:17:

> *Herein is our love made perfect, that we may have boldness in the day of judgment: because as he is, so are we in this world.*

This isn't saying that someday in heaven we will be like Jesus; it's saying that we are as He is...NOW...IN THIS WORLD! This is who we are. We didn't get lost; we don't have to find ourselves; we have already been found by Jesus Christ, and He is living inside of us. The only way for us to really know and understand this is from divine revelation from God. Ask Him for it; He is more than ready to reveal to you the magnificence of His presence in you.

God has a plan for each of us—handpicked for us as individuals. There are some who reject God's plan, which results in Him choosing someone else, but there are also times when, if we don't carry out that plan, it won't be accomplished. This was said of John the Baptist in Malachi 4:6.

> *And he shall turn the heart of the fathers to the children, and the heart of the children to their fathers, lest I come and smite the earth with a curse.*

If John the Baptist had not fulfilled his mission, then the earth would be cursed! There would be no salvation for us! This means that God did not have a second choice standing by. It was John or no one.

I believe that unless we are fulfilling God's plan for our lives, we will feel empty, like we are missing something. When we are not right smack in the middle of God's plan, we can become depressed with life and find ourselves looking in all different directions for the answer. We feel confused. But the answer has been inside of us all along.

When I was raising my children, there were times that I looked forward to the plan God had for me. But the Lord showed me that raising my children in the nurture and admonition of the Lord *was* His plan for me during that season of my life. He showed me that being their mom *was* my ministry. In fact, other than being a help mate to my husband, it was the most important thing I could be doing at that time. Once I understood that I became content and focused. While we are busy with our families, we seem to want to rush this time so we can get on with other things, but in doing so, we miss the very special, once-in-a-lifetime opportunity to impact the lives of our children with the Word of God.

The fact is, we *are* to invest our lives into our children; we *are* to give of ourselves to them. But to say that once they are grown, I can get on with my life and find myself, is saying that raising them was not as important as what's coming next. We need to treasure the privilege of raising godly children.

We need to remember *who* we are in Christ and the power that has been given to us, and then when we feel overwhelmed or not appreciated, or confused regarding our identity, we can look to the One who is living inside of us and be reminded of who we really are in Him. Then we can look forward to the next phase of His awesome plan for us.

Once we remember this, we can rise up as warriors and fight the good fight of faith, renouncing every evil thought that comes to us that says we have no value or worth.

Rise up and speak, "I am the righteousness of God (Eph. 4:24); I am fulfilling God's plan and purpose for me (Jer. 29:11); I have the mind of Christ (1 Cor. 2:16); I am a new creature in Christ (2 Cor. 5:17); as He is, so am I in this world (1 John 4:17); I walk in newness of life (Rom. 6:4); I am victorious (1 Cor. 15:57); I am more than a conqueror (Rom. 8:38); I have peace because my mind stays on the Lord, and I trust in Him (Isa. 26:3); I can do all things through Christ who strengthens me (Phil. 4:13); I will not grow weary in doing good, for in due season I shall reap (Gal. 6:9); I have overcome the world (1 John 5:4); I am walking by faith and not by sight (2 Cor. 5:7)."

Give thanks to God for His awesome plan and perfect love for us!

Chapter Two

Blessed to Be a Blessing

And I will make of thee a great nation, and I will bless thee, and make thy name great; and thou shalt be a blessing.

Genesis 12:2

We are blessed! The Bible tells us so.

> *Blessed be the God and Father of our Lord Jesus Christ, who hath blessed us with all spiritual blessings in heavenly places in Christ. Ephesians 1:3*

Whether we feel like it or not and whether we can see blessings in our lives or not doesn't change the truth that we are blessed. It is, of course, God's desire that we walk, live in, and see these blessings in our everyday lives, but unfortunately this is not necessarily the case with some Christians. Some lack knowledge regarding God's desire to bless us, while others just don't believe that life can be that good.

Before we discover why God chose to bless His people, let's look at some signs of being blessed. Blessed people walk in health; they are prosperous; they are delivered from addictions, bondages, and all harm; they are forgiven, and they know it; everything their hand touches prospers and is successful; they are happy, peaceful, and joyful; their children are happy, healthy, and a joy and blessing to their parents; they have healthy relationships.

As Christians, it is so important that we know, understand, and believe that we are blessed and that we live in these blessings daily. Why did God bless us in the first place, and why is it so important that we know it? It's out of His love for us that we are blessed. God always has a purpose for what He does, and everything He does flows out of His unconditional love.

I believe there are two reasons why He wants us to believe in and experience His blessings. The first is so we can bring attention to Him. God's blessings are a witness to a lost and dying world that He exists and is good. Second, He blesses us so that we can bless others.

God told Abraham, *I will make of thee a great nation,*

and I will bless thee, and make thy name great; and thou shalt be a blessing (Gen. 12:2). Abraham was about to be blessed so that he could bless others. We must understand and live in these blessings ourselves in order to bless others because we can't give away what we don't have.

In Matthew 25, Jesus talks about the Shepherd dividing His sheep from the goats. The sheep represent those who honored the Lord during their lives, and the goats symbolize those who did not.

> *And he shall set the sheep on his right hand, but the goats on the left. Then shall the King say unto them on his right hand, Come, ye blessed of my Father, inherit the kingdom prepared for you from the foundation of the world. For I was an hungred, and ye gave me meat: I was thirsty, and ye gave me drink: I was a stranger, and ye took me in. Naked, and ye clothed me: I was sick, and ye visited me: I was in prison, and ye came unto me. (vv. 33-36)*

Jesus called His sheep blessed. They were not only blessed as they stood before Him, but they were blessed in their lives on earth. They believed they were blessed and lived it! So what did they do with what they had? They didn't keep it for themselves; they understood that their blessings were meant for others. They fed those who were hungry and gave drink to those who were thirsty. Notice that the scripture doesn't say the hungry person asked for food.

My husband and I can notice when people are hungry and need food or drink, even when they don't say anything to us. Does that mean that because they don't ask for anything we don't meet their need? No, of course not. That would be like saying we don't need to forgive those who don't ask to be forgiven. Because these people had been blessed by God with food and drink, they blessed others with the same.

One day, on my way to the grocery store, the Lord prompted me to pray. When I arrived at the store, I noticed a young woman who appeared to be in need. It was a very cold day, and she was without a jacket and wearing shorts. She looked desperate and in a rush as she tried to balance many items in her arms. I waited a few moments to consider her. (*Blessed is he that considereth the poor... Ps. 41:1.*) Then I met her need by paying for her groceries. I was able to bless her, so I did.

In Matthew 25, the sheep also gave shelter to the homeless. There are many homeless people in the world. If we know of one, but can't take that person into our home, then we can certainly direct him or her to a shelter.

These sheep also clothed the naked. They either gave away their clothes, made clothing for those who had none, or purchased some for them. I listen to people when they talk. If I hear them talking about one of their favorite clothing stores, and I know they seldom shop there because of limited finances, I keep that in mind and purchase a gift card to that store for them.

The sheep also visited the sick and those in prison. Giving of your time is just as important as giving of your resources. There was a lady I was introduced to years ago, and I was asked to pray with her because she had a disease for many years. I visited this woman for two years on a weekly basis, praying and ministering to her. Her condition worsened by the day. There were times I just sat there as she was sleeping; I wasn't even sure she knew I was there, but it didn't matter. I gave of my time.

I must admit I had never visited anyone in prison. For a while, it concerned me because my desire was to fulfill this passage. I asked the Lord to open up an opportunity where I could do that. Two weeks later, a chaplain from the local jail approached me and asked if she could purchase some of our books. What an opportunity! We donated a carton of books, and they were distributed throughout the jail. God spoke to my heart at a later date showing me how we have indeed visited those in prison. God has such wonderful ways of doing things!

Continuing in Matthew 25, we learn about the goats.

Then shall he say also unto them on the left hand, Depart from me, ye cursed, into everlasting fire, prepared for the devil and his angels: For I was an hungred, and ye gave me no meat: I was thirsty, and ye gave me no drink: I was a stranger, and ye took me not in: naked, and ye clothed me not: sick, and in prison, and ye visited me not. Then shall they also answer him, saying, Lord, when saw we thee an hungred, or athirst, or a stranger, or naked, or sick, or in prison, and did not minister unto thee? Then shall he answer them, saying, Verily I say unto you, Inasmuch

> *as ye did it not to one of the least of these, ye did it not to me. (vv. 41-45)*

During their lives on earth the goats saw people who were hungry and thirsty, naked, and without shelter; they knew of those in jail or of those who were sick, yet they did NOTHING! These are the greedy ones who kept everything they had to themselves. They either didn't realize that all they had came from God, or they just didn't care. Jesus called them cursed.

Notice how important blessing others is to Jesus:

> *Inasmuch as ye have done it unto the least of these my brethren, ye have done it unto me. (v. 40)*

WOW! Whatever good we do to others, we are doing to Jesus Himself! But the reverse is just as true:

> *Inasmuch as ye did it NOT to one of the least of these, ye did it NOT to me. (v. 45, emphasis mine)*

Jesus is saying that what we do or don't do to others, we do or don't do to Him—or the way we treat others is the way we treat Him! Jesus takes blessing others very seriously and personally.

At this point you may be thinking that you don't have very much to give, but everyone has something. There is always something we can do or give, even if we have little. In Luke 21 Jesus commends the poor widow:

> *Looking up, [Jesus] saw the rich people putting their gifts into the treasury. And He saw also a poor widow putting in two mites (copper coins). And He said, Truly I say to you, this poor widow has put in more than all of them; For they all gave out of their abundance (their surplus); but she has contributed out of her lack and her want, putting in all that she had on which to live. (vv. 1-4, The Amplified Bible)*

Jesus saw what she gave as more than all the rich people combined. Why? Because it was a sacrifice on her part. She blessed Jesus with what she had even if it was just two coins. This should be an encouragement to us that whatever we give—big or small—if we give it cheerfully, God considers it great! (See 2 Cor. 9:7.)

Even if we start out small and give out of our lack, He will increase it back to us. Second Corinthians 9:10 says that God gives seed to the sower. He will get the money *to* us because He can get it *through* us. He knows He can trust us to give it out again. Starting out small is much better than not starting at all, and if we will keep it going, we will eventually get to a place where we should all be: where it is no longer a sacrifice because we have so much, we can keep on blessing others.

> *And God is able to make all grace abound toward you; that ye, always having all sufficiency in all things, may abound to every good work. 2 Corinthians 9:8*

There will be no lack when it comes to helping others! If we give of our time, we will have so much time on our hands we won't know what to do with it. Same with our resources. I heard someone say that we are to operate like distribution centers: the money comes in, the money goes out; more money comes in, more money goes out! (See Luke 6:38.) Everyone wins this way. People's needs are met, we become prosperous, and God gets the glory that He deserves.

Chapter Three

Following Jesus

Be ye therefore followers of God, as dear children.

Ephesians 5:1

There is a difference between being born again and being a follower of God. Most people would read the above verse and feel very satisfied with themselves because they believe by being born again they are automatically followers of God. But this is not what Scripture teaches; there is a difference.

Being born again begins with realizing we need a Savior and, by faith, believing and receiving all that Jesus has done for us through His grace. But the original Greek meaning of the word *follower* in Ephesians 5:1 is "to imitate." We can conclude then, that being born again is just the beginning, and being a follower of God is the continuation of that commitment.

Notice that verse 1 begins, *Be ye therefore...* The word *therefore* makes it clear that we should connect this verse with the prior verses in Ephesians 4.

> *If so be that ye have heard him, and have been taught by him, as the truth is in Jesus. Ephesians 4:21*

This is referring to someone who is in Christ or who has been born again. Ephesians 4:22 and on show us those things that should manifest in our lives as a result of becoming a new creation. These verses tell us to put off our old lifestyle, indicating that we could still be in our old lifestyle even though we are saved. This is because it is by faith that we are saved, not works. When people get saved, they don't immediately change. I like what Bible teacher Andrew Wommack says: "If you were skinny before you got saved, then you'll be skinny after you get saved, or if you were smart before you got saved then you'll be smart after you get saved." Colossians 3:1-8 further confirm the putting off of our old lifestyle.

> *If ye then be risen with Christ, seek those things which are above, where Christ sitteth on the right hand of God. Set your affection on things above, not on things*

on the earth. For ye are dead, and your life is hid with Christ in God. When Christ, who is our life, shall appear, then shall ye also appear with him in glory. Mortify therefore your members which are upon the earth; fornication, uncleanness, inordinate affection, evil concupiscence, and covetousness, which is idolatry: For which things' sake the wrath of God cometh on the children of disobedience: In the which ye also walked some time, when ye lived in them. But now ye also put off all these; anger, wrath, malice, blasphemy, filthy communication out of your mouth.

Now that we are in Christ we should start imitating Him with our lifestyle. Our ways need to change, but it's now possible because of the empowerment of the Holy Spirit! But it's a process to change, and many remain in their former lifestyle for years before they move on, which is a choice of their own.

Someone once told me that we can have as much of God as we want. And, I would add, as quickly as we want! Bible teacher Joyce Meyer said that she became born again, but it took her years to finally be led by the Spirit. This wasn't God's fault; it was her decision.

Ephesians 4 continues to exhort us to put off lusting of any kind, to be renewed in our minds, and to put on righteousness and holiness (vv. 22-24); to put away lying, but speak to the truth (v. 25); to stop stealing, but to work instead (v. 28); to watch our words and only speak that which will edify one another (v. 29); to put away all bitterness, wrath, anger, clamor, evil speaking, and malice, and rather to be kind to one another, tender hearted, and forgiving (v. 31-32).

These passages involve a lot of "what to do and what not to do." Sounds like the Law, doesn't it? We know we are free from the Law or from keeping the Law to gain God's approval, so what do these passages mean?

Remember that verse 21 speaks of hearing and accepting Jesus. If we truly understand who we are in Christ and renew our minds to that truth and to the mercy, goodness, and grace of God, then we won't want to do these things. When I think about how good God is to me and how much He loves me, it makes me want to please Him even more! Grace teaches us to deny ungodliness; it doesn't make us want to sin.

For the grace of God that bringeth salvation hath appeared to all men, Teaching us that, denying ungodliness and worldly lusts, we should live soberly, righteously, and godly, in this present world. Titus 2:11-12

God's grace and goodness make us want to deny anything ungodly. There is a balance between grace and faith, and whether we like it or not, there are things we must do or not do in order to take advantage of the blessed life. And we now have the Holy Spirit, who empowers us to forsake our former lifestyle.

These prior passages have nothing to do with following the rules so that God will love us or accept us more. We are as loved and as accepted as we'll ever be. Following these precepts does not change God one bit, but it does benefit us. This is the reason Paul exhorts us to live a godly life. It's just plain smart.

It also pleases God when we live right. It's almost an "extra" for Him, if you will. God is never mad at us; He is never disappointed in us, because He is looking at us through His Son, Jesus. He can't be upset with us in any way. But when we live godly, as these scriptures teach,

He gets extra pleasure from it—maybe super excited and jumping for joy!

Ephesians 5:10 says that when we walk as children of the light, we *prove what is acceptable to the Lord.* The word *acceptable* translates into "well pleasing"!

> *And whatsoever we ask, we receive of him, because we keep his commandments, and do those things that are PLEASING in his sight. 1 John 3:22 (emphasis mine)*

In Philippians 4:18 Paul is thanking the Philippians for everything he received from them, and he calls their giving *a sacrifice WELL PLEASING to the Lord.*

So, although our lifestyle does not change God's love for us, it does change us, and it pleases God. This is why we should heed the urgings in Scripture. We as Christians should want to please God.

In Ephesians 5 we can see the first example of God's heart when it comes to being a follower.

> *And walk in love, as Christ also hath loved us, and*

hath given himself for us an offering and a sacrifice to God for a sweet smelling savour. (v. 2)

Lying to someone is not the way to love that person, white lies included. White has always been the color of innocence, righteousness, goodness, and purity, but there is nothing pure about a lie, no matter how big or small. To make people feel foolish or mad because they were lied to is not loving them.

Stealing is also not based on love. People are affected when you steal from them. They are violated, and they feel it. They no longer have what was stolen from them and may even have to replace it, which would cost money. How is this loving them?

Corrupt communication is not love. Why? Because others are hearing it and are affected by it. The meaning of the word *corrupt* is "poor quality, bad, unfit for use, worthless."

Bitterness, wrath, anger, clamor, evil speaking, and malice are not love. Fornication, uncleanness, covetousness, filthiness, foolish talking or jesting, and idolatry are not love (see vv. 3-5).

This type of lifestyle doesn't only affect you, but it affects others, and that is not walking in love. Romans 13:10 says that *love worketh no ill to his neighbour.* If we love God like we say we do, then walking in love toward others is proof of it.

Would God do any of the above? No. He is love and therefore only acts with love. Because we claim to be His followers, we need to imitate Him.

Here is a simple example of truly imitating God by walking in love. Luke 6:28 tells us to bless those who curse us. God is telling us to do something. The word *bless* is an action word. I once bought a gift for someone who offended me. This was my first experience of really blessing someone who was my enemy. I can recall driving to the mall to purchase a gift and realizing that it was the very first time I did NOT want to go to the mall! I love the mall, but I dreaded this trip. I purchased a gift, bought a card, and wrapped the gift beautifully. I gave it to the person who offended me, and I cannot express the pleasure I felt from the Lord. It brought joy to me, which made it easier to do the next time (see Neh. 8:10).

The big question is, why does God want us to imitate Him? Is it an ego trip of His? Is He just a hard taskmaster who wants to make it difficult for us? Galatians 5:16-21 is full of even more unfit behavior, but then concludes with, *they which do such things shall not inherit the kingdom of God.* This does not mean we won't go to heaven; it simply means we will not experience the kingdom that's already in us...it won't manifest in our lives!

God wants us to experience all that we received from Him when we received Jesus. When we do we will be right in the middle of the abundant life Jesus died to give us. Let's imitate Jesus, walking in love in all we say and all we do. Then we will be true followers of God!

Chapter Four

God's "To-Do" List

Verily I say unto you, Whatsoever ye shall bind on earth shall be bound in heaven: and whatsoever ye shall loose on earth shall be loosed in heaven.

Matthew 18:18

"Dear God, please be with us today. Dear God, give me Your peace. Dear God, heal my disease. Dear God, help me not to worry. Dear God, please protect me. Dear God, please take this problem from me. Dear God, please get the devil off my back. Oh Lord, please forgive me. Bless me today. Dear Lord, please give me more faith."

Have you ever heard these prayers from others, or have you ever said them yourself? This is the way I used to pray before I became born again, and even some years after.

I had been taught that whatever I needed, I could ask God, and He would give it to me because He loved me. But

I noticed that nothing really changed; it was as if God wasn't hearing me, or if He did hear me, He just decided at times not to answer. I was also told that sometimes God says yes, and sometimes God says no. But there was something I did not know. There was a lack of knowledge on my part, but when I received revelation on why these kinds of prayers were not working, I changed my thinking as fast as I could.

I realized that the knowledge I *did* have was incorrect. It was wrong information that could have eventually made my life miserable here on this earth. In Hosea 4:6 God says, *My people are destroyed for lack of knowledge: because thou hast rejected knowledge.*

But then I learned about the finished work of Jesus Christ. This was a major turning point in my life. Until then, I had no idea exactly what was accomplished at the cross 2,000 years ago. I thought, as many do today, that Jesus died to forgive me of my sins so I could go to heaven someday. That's correct, and thank God for salvation, but that was all I knew about why Jesus died. I knew nothing of the healing, the prosperity, the deliverance, the protection, the wholeness, and the abundant life that Christ died to give us.

To know that Jesus died so that we could be forgiven and also able to walk in health because He took all of our sicknesses and diseases onto His own body, opened up a whole new world for me. I began realizing that the reason I wasn't getting healed in certain areas when I asked God to heal me was simply because He had already healed me 2,000 years ago! I just didn't know it. I didn't know what I already had available to me.

Recently my husband and I made plane reservations for a four-hour flight across the country. We purchased two seats in coach, which is what we always do, but then as we got closer to the day of the flight, we received an email asking if we wanted to be put onto a list for first-class seats. If we got the seats, it would cost an additional $450. We signed on only because it was a long flight.

When we hadn't heard anything from the airline, I called them for the status. The operator asked me if I had a Dividend Miles card, which I did. I barely use the card so I forgot I had it until she asked me. She searched for a few minutes then informed me that we had 35,000 dividend miles on the card. Because of that, we could move up to first class for only $75! Needless to say, we upgraded and had a wonderful flight.

I barely remembered I even had a card and certainly had no knowledge that I was accumulating miles to put toward first-class seats one day, among other benefits. It was a lack of knowledge on my part of what I already had. Because I didn't know what I had, I could have missed a great blessing!

It's the same with us as Christians. If we don't know what we have already been given, we will be asking God for things we already have. We try to get God to do something for us that we think He hasn't done yet. This is incorrect. God has done absolutely everything He will ever do! He moved ONCE and for all (see Heb. 10:10). It was all done at the cross 2,000 years ago.

The Greek word *sozo* has been translated to mean "save" or "saved," which refers to salvation. But it also translates to "physical healing" (see Mark 5:23 and Acts 14:8-10) and to "be made whole," referring to healing in every way—physically and emotionally (see Luke 8:50). The word also applies to deliverance from demons (see Luke 8:36). And 2 Corinthians 8:9 makes it clear that we are redeemed from poverty!

It's obvious from the Word of God that salvation encompasses everything—forgiveness of sins, physical healing, deliverance, prosperity, wholeness, and completeness, yet we keep asking God for these things as if we don't have them, but we *do* have them! He can't answer prayers He's already answered, and He can't say no to what He's already said yes to! We just need to apply our faith to allow the things that have been given to us by His grace to be released in our lives.

My husband, Al, had a vision awhile back where he saw God in the center of thousands of people. They were all praying. Their prayers were going upward toward the face of God, but their prayers passed right by Him and continued in an upright position. God wasn't answering them; it was as if He couldn't even hear them.

Al asked the Lord to show him the meaning of the vision. God showed him that His children were asking Him for things He already gave them, and they were asking Him to do things He had told them to do.

Why ask God to heal us when Matthew 8:17 states: *That it might be fulfilled which was spoken by Esaias the prophet, saying, Himself took our infirmities, [weakness and pain], and bare our sicknesses (brackets mine)*?

Why ask God to forgive us when Hebrews 10:12 says: *But this man, after he had offered one sacrifice for sins forever*?

Why ask God to be with you when Hebrews 13:5 promises: *I will never leave thee, nor forsake thee*?

Why ask God to bless us when Ephesians 1:3 tells us: *Blessed be the God and Father of our Lord Jesus Christ, who hath blessed us with all spiritual blessings in heavenly places in Christ*?

Why ask God to give us faith when Galatians 2:20 says: *I am crucified with Christ: nevertheless I live; yet not I, but Christ liveth in me: and the life which I now live in the flesh I live by the faith of the Son of God, who loved me, and gave himself for me*?

Rather than asking God to do what He has already done, we should be thanking Him for what He has done, and then, by faith, releasing those things into our physical lives.

For example, if someone was in financial trouble, rather than asking God to provide money, he should purposefully tithe from what he already has, expecting it to come back to him 100 times over (see Matt.13:8). That person should then pray something like, "Lord, I have put this money into Your kingdom with a cheerful heart, and according to Your Word, I will receive back 100 fold. I expect increase in my finances. Thank You, Lord, that Your Word is true when it says: *Give and it shall be given unto you; good measure, pressed down, shaken together, and running over, shall men give into [my] bosom (Luke 6:38, brackets mine).*

This is how we can use our faith to release the blessing of prosperity! When we speak like this, heaven hears it. Matthew 18:18 tells us that whatever we bind on earth will be bound in heaven, and whatever we loose on earth will be loosed in heaven. In its context, this scripture is referring to church discipline, but we can certainly apply it to other areas in our lives. Heaven is just waiting to hear what we have to say about the matter. And once we say it, whether we are binding or loosing, it will come to pass.

The devil is behind all evil, whether directly or indirectly. There are some who ask God to get the devil off their back.

But, again, God has told us to do it. He has given us authority over all the wiles of the evil one. We are not to fight the devil in the sense that we try to win, because he has already been defeated in our lives. We are to stand on the Word of God, being sober and vigilant, defending what is rightfully ours (see 1 Peter 5:8).

I heard a Bible teacher tell the story of his visit to Buckingham Palace in England. He noticed soldiers standing in front of the palace, not saying anything; they were just standing holding their weapons. They weren't fighting, just standing. They were protecting what they already owned: their land. The fight for the land was won years before; now they are just carefully guarding what's already in their possession! They were being sober and vigilant. Spiritually, our battle has been won; all we need to do is to be sober and vigilant as we defend what is rightfully ours, what has been given to us because of the grace of God.

If we want results in our lives, we have to understand WHO we are in Christ, WHAT we have in Him, and HOW to use what we have been given. Once we realize these things, we will then understand why our prayers never seem to get answered. We will see that we are asking for something we already have, or we are asking God to do something He already did, or something He told us to do. God has done all that He's ever going to do. It's up to us, His children, to take the reins and assume control over our lives with His Word as our foundation.

Chapter Five

Got Humility?

Humble yourselves therefore under the mighty hand of God, that he may exalt you in due time.

1 Peter 5:6

Humility is a word that tends to invoke a feeling of inferiority or low self-esteem. It's a hard word for some, and at times brings fear of possibly being "stepped on" in life. When I discovered the true biblical meaning of humility, however, it brought me freedom, along with a greater understanding of the positive effects of living humbly.

First Peter 5:6 tells us that we need to humble ourselves so that God can exalt us. But let's back up to verses 1-3, which show us what true humility is. These verses are directed to church elders, those mature in the Lord:

> *The elders which are among you I exhort, who am also an elder, and a witness of the sufferings of Christ, and*

also a partaker of the glory that shall be revealed: Feed the flock of God which is among you, taking the oversight thereof, not by constraint, but willingly; not for filthy lucre, but of a ready mind; Neither as being lords over God's heritage, but being examples to the flock.

These are specific instructions on how we should treat those we minister to. We are to gently feed them or look after them willingly and not with the motive of making money, but from a heart of love and concern. We are not to "lord" over them, being forceful, but should lead by example.

Verse 5 is directed to those who are younger, who are learning from their elders. Peter tells them to submit to their elders.

Likewise, ye younger, submit yourselves unto the elder. Yea, all of you be subject one to another, and be clothed with humility: for God resisteth the proud, and giveth grace to the humble.

Peter wants us to know that whether we are elders, or learning from an elder, we need to be humble and subject to one another. We are all called to humility. Notice that

1 Peter 5:5 says that God resists the proud. One of the Greek meanings for the word *resist* is "to oppose." But if we are humble, God gives us grace, which in the Greek means "goodwill, that which affords joy, pleasure, delight, sweetness, loveliness." Such opposites!

Verse 6 continues:

> *Humble yourselves therefore under the mighty hand of God, that he may exalt you in due time.*

All of the above scriptures continually exhort us to be humble, but how are we to do that? First Peter 5:7 reveals the way.

> *Casting all your care upon him; for he careth for you.*

What an awesome scripture! We have all cast our care onto the Lord at some point in our lives; I have, you have, and even Jesus did. In 1 Peter 2:23, Jesus cast His care onto His Father:

> *Who, when he was reviled, reviled not again; when he suffered, he threatened not; but committed himself to him that judgeth righteously.*

I've always admired those who knew how to cast their cares. They would have a major need but seemed to have no problem giving it all to Jesus. I would ask them how things were going, and they would simply say, "Oh, God's got that covered; I cast my care on Him." I was always impressed that some could do that and not be concerned any longer about their situation.

But I noticed something as time went on. Months or even years later these same people would still be waiting for their answer. Their problem was still there, maybe even a bit worse, yet they were still casting their care. It seemed to me that it wasn't working, which prompted me to look further into Scripture. I didn't have to look very far.

> *...Casting all your care upon him; for he careth for you. Be sober, be vigilant; because your adversary the devil, as a roaring lion, walketh about, seeking whom he may devour: Whom resist stedfast in the faith, knowing that the same afflictions are accomplished in your brethren that are in the world. 1 Peter 5:7-8*

Although "same afflictions" is referring to persecution, this truth can apply to any trial in our lives. Look at the following meanings: *be sober*—"to watch"; *be vigilant*—"to keep awake or be watchful"; *stedfast in the faith*—"solid, sure, and strong." It's not enough to just cast our care; we also need to fight!

> *For this purpose the Son of God was manifested, that he might destroy the works of the devil. 1 John 3:8b*

Jesus already destroyed the works of the devil. It was done at the cross, but the devil doesn't want you to know that. He'll try to mess with your mind to get you to think otherwise, to get you to think that God's Word is not true. Whenever a trial comes into our lives, he gets into our thinking to create fear and worry. This is the time to fight. Not with one another, but in the spiritual realm with right thinking and right speaking.

Remember when Jesus looked at Peter but spoke to the devil, saying, *Get thee behind me, Satan (Matt. 16:23)*? We must remember this because too many times we spend hours talking about the person who has offended us. We become very angry and even tell that person off, but it's actually Satan who's behind the entire thing.

In Ephesians 1 we learn about our inheritance in Christ and the exceeding power we have been given—the same power that raised Jesus from the dead. It's inside of us! It tells us how we are above all principalities and powers and explains that all things are under our feet. As Christians, we need to know who we are and what we have (see Phile. 6).

Once we're convinced of who we are in Christ, we can obey the instruction of Ephesians 4:26-27, which tells us to *be ye angry and sin not: let not the sun go down upon your wrath: neither give place to the devil.* What this does *not* mean is that we must make sure we don't go to bed at night angry at someone. It doesn't mean that we should make peace with everyone before we turn in for the night. Of course, it's good that we don't go to bed angry, but this is not what this verse means.

This has always been a very misunderstood scripture. It's not talking about our anger with people; it's talking about our anger toward the devil! To *not* be angry at the devil is wrong. This verse is instructing us to never give up on being angry with the devil. We must be relentless. It's a matter of what we want in life and how much we really want it.

Similarly, in Matthew 11:12 we learn that *the kingdom of heaven suffereth violence, and the violent take it by force.* This means we must forcefully press into the Gospel. We must be aggressive in overcoming obstacles in our lives. Casting our care upon the Lord is not enough.

Although Florida is beautiful, it is a prime target for hurricanes. We suffered three major hurricanes within two years. While many were preparing for the storm, I walked around my property and spoke protection over everything we owned. As a result, there was never any damage, praise the Lord. After the third storm, I realized I could take authority over them. So I began aggressively fighting against any storm by speaking to it. I was just tired of these storms putting a stop to normal everyday living. It was time to step up the battle plan. It's now been nine years, and we haven't had another hurricane in our town since. (You can read more of this story and others in our book, *God's Best Is for You TOO!*) If I just cast my care onto the Lord and didn't fight, I can guarantee that every storm headed our way would have made it to Florida!

You might be thinking at this point that I got off-track from talking about humility, but I didn't. It is true that casting our care is a sign of humility, but fighting is also a sign of humility. Why? Because it's what God says to do. When we are passive and don't take our authority, we are not doing it God's way, and that's arrogance. God Himself told us to be strong in the faith, so when we obey Him, we are being humble.

Jesus is called the Lion of the tribe of Judah in Revelation 5. Lions are powerful, bold, and strong. He is also called the Lamb of God. Lambs are gentle. We as Christians should be gentle as lambs, casting our care onto the Lord by allowing Him to get involved in our situations rather than "we" trying to fix them. At the same time we need to be as bold as lions, coming boldly to the throne of grace (see Heb. 4:16), taking our authority in the unseen world to defend what is rightfully ours, which is peace, joy, healing, deliverance, protection, and wholeness. And that, my brothers and sisters, is true humility.

Chapter Six

He Took the Real Thing

And ye are complete in him, which is the head of all principality and power.

Colossians 2:10

Recently I was meditating on the resurrection of Jesus Christ, and I began thinking how I would minister the power of the Resurrection to others. Many of the churches I've attended on Easter Sunday take this opportunity to evangelize people to receive Jesus as their Lord and Savior. That's great and wonderful. I'm all for that, especially since there are many who do not attend church on a regular basis except for special holidays. I believe it's a great opportunity for ministers to share the salvation message. I began wondering how I could lead up to this great message of eternal life.

It's true that Jesus died to forgive us of our sins:

For this is my blood of the new testament, which is shed for many for the remission of sins. Matthew 26:28

There is no other way to receive forgiveness of sin but through the blood of Jesus. I will always be grateful that Jesus willingly laid down His life so I could be forgiven of my sin and go to heaven someday.

Matthew 1:21 states, *She shall bring forth a son, and thou shalt call his name Jesus: for he shall save his people from their sins.* There is only one sin that can keep us out of heaven, and that is the sin of not believing in Jesus. But this is not the only reason Jesus died.

Forgiveness of sin is vital; without it, we would spend eternity in hell. But there are many more reasons why Jesus died, and it's important to include all of them when ministering to others. We must be sure to preach the entire Gospel (Good News) and not just part of it. What is the entire Gospel? The following was accomplished on our behalf 2,000 years ago:

Deliverance—Jesus died so we could be delivered. Delivered from what? From the devil's hold on us or from demonic activity in our lives.

In Luke 8:33 Jesus met a demon-possessed man with many demons. Jesus commanded the demons to leave, and they did. *Then went the devils out of the man (v. 33).* Jesus was teaching His disciples that once they received the Holy Spirit, they too could deliver others from demons. More importantly, we must understand that Jesus *wanted* the man free.

When Jesus hung on the cross He yelled out, *It is finished* (see John 19:30). He meant that we are now free from all demonic bondage, fear, worry, anxiety, confusion, addictions, loneliness, pain, grief, and so on. Jesus bore it *all* for us.

Protection—Psalm 91 is a beautiful picture of God's protection. We do not have to ask God to protect us because He already is! We just need to believe it is happening. He also protects anything that concerns us, such as our children, our families, our assets, and so forth.

> *The angel of the Lord encampeth round about them that fear him, and delivereth them. Psalm 34:7*

One of the meanings of the word *encampeth* is "to pitch a tent." Our angels aren't going anywhere, and they deliver us! We won't see this protection manifest in our lives, or only to a small extent, if we don't believe God will do it. And what we don't believe, we don't expect will happen.

Our expecting has to be done on purpose, just like everything else. An example is in the area of giving. If we don't give with purpose, expecting a harvest, it will not be given back to us. We can give and give and give, but it has to be done with purpose and expectation. It's the same with protection. God's Word promises us protection, but will we believe and expect that protection?

Prosperity—Jesus took our poverty onto the cross.

For ye know the grace of our Lord Jesus Christ, that, though he was rich, yet for your sakes he became poor, that ye through his poverty might be rich. 2 Corinthians 8:9

This word *rich* in the original Greek translates to "have abundance in outward possessions, to be richly supplied, affluent in resources so that you can be a blessing to all."

This is talking about MONEY! I agree with those who say that we are made rich in the beautiful character of the Lord, but this is *not* what this verse is talking about. It's referring to us being prosperous in money and possessions so that we can help others. Jesus died so we could be financially prosperous.

Physical Healing—This is the area that many people struggle with the most.

> *And the prayer of faith shall save the sick, and the Lord shall raise him up. James 5:15*

The word *save* in the Greek translates to "sozo," which means physical healing. Often in the Bible, *save* or *saved,* translate to "sozo," which means that salvation, which came at Jesus' death on the cross, covers everything, including physical healing!

Acts 3:1-9 tell the story of Peter and John going to the temple. At the temple gate, they were asked by a certain lame man if they had money. Peter fastened his eyes on the man and told him he had no silver or gold, but what he *did* have he would give to him.

And he took him by the right hand, and lifted him up: and immediately his feet and ankle bones received strength. And he leaping up stood, and walked, and entered with them into the temple, walking, and leaping, and praising God! (vv. 7-8)

Almost every sermon I've heard on this passage said that this was talking about a spiritual healing and that this is where the man became born again. Maybe he did get saved, but he was also 100 percent physically healed!

That's why he was walking and leaping—something he could not have done before. If we can't believe that this man was physically healed, then we will never believe that we can be! The Word of God means what it says!

Sickness is a curse (see Deut. 28). In Deuteronomy God makes a distinction between blessings and curses, and sickness is listed under the curses. But we have been redeemed from the curse; from sickness and disease. We have even been redeemed from a hangnail!

Bless the LORD, *O my soul, and forget not all his benefits: Who forgiveth all thine iniquities; who healeth all thy diseases. Psalm 103:2-3*

Notice that forgiveness of sins and healing are in the same sentence. You can't have one without the other. The Lord showed me something that may help us understand what was actually accomplished on the cross. Last year I received a beautiful designer purse as a gift. I was a bit shocked because I knew the cost of this purse, as I had admired it previously. But I also was very pleased I received it. A couple of months later while I was visiting a friend, I noticed that she had the exact same purse. (Because of the cost, these purses are not that common.)

We laughed and began talking about how expensive they were. To my surprise she told me she bought hers for only $29! My mouth dropped open. My purse cost over $150! But then she told me that it was a knock-off, or an imitation, of the real designer purse. Amazingly, they both looked alike in every way. Yet, I had the real thing, and she didn't.

God was showing me that His Son took the real sickness (or pain, fear, or confusion) onto Himself 2,000 years ago; therefore, those who are sick are actually experiencing an imitation of the sickness! The symptoms are just lies of the enemy to trick us into thinking that we are sick and that God's Word is not true. The sickness He took and the symptoms we may have look exactly alike, but what we are experiencing is a fake because Jesus took the real sicknesses upon Himself.

When I received this revelation, I got angry—not at God—at the devil, the one behind it all. John 10:10 tells us:

> *The thief cometh not, but for to steal, and to kill, and to destroy: I am come that they might have life, and that they might have it more abundantly.*

People aren't walking in divine health simply because they do not believe in the finished work of Jesus Christ. They believe they can be well sometime in the future, but they don't believe they have already been made well. It ALREADY happened. The Gospel is past tense! Jesus took all of our symptoms so that we don't have to experience any of them—ever! Once we receive a revelation of His finished work, we will begin to walk in all of His benefits.

This was Paul's prayer in the first chapter of Ephesians 1:17-23. He prayed that God's children would see their benefits—what their true inheritance is in Him—including physical healing.

Because of this truth, we need to come to God—not as the sick trying to get well, but as the healed fighting off the symptoms or lies that are coming against us, and we need to defend what is rightfully ours, which is our divine health. Symptoms have no right to take over our bodies because He took it all for us. This is why the body of Jesus was so beaten and bruised beyond recognition. He carried tumors, cancers, addictions, and pain for us so we would never have to carry them. This is love. Thank You, Jesus.

When symptoms try to attack our bodies, we need to take the authority that Jesus gave us (see Luke 9:1) and command all that is not of God to leave our bodies, then release healing from our Spirit man into our physical bodies.

I'm sure now we can understand why the Gospel is called Good News. It's good news to be forgiven, healed, delivered, protected, and prosperous. This is the entire Gospel.

And of his fulness have all we received. John 1:16

Chapter Seven

Jesus, the Center of It All

For in him we live, and move, and have our being; as certain also of your own poets have said, For we are also his offspring.

Acts 17:28

Have you ever heard anyone use the phrase, "It's the principle of the thing?" Or have you ever said it yourself? I certainly have until God gave me great revelation on this very statement. Let's look at two examples where people might declare, "It's the principle of the thing!"

There's going to be a party in your neighborhood next week. You know about it because everyone got an invitation...except you. You know you should have been invited because, after all, you introduced many of your neighbors to each other. You begin to wonder why you weren't invited. You know you wouldn't be able to attend the party anyway because you had other plans on that day, but, "It's the principle of the thing!" You should have been invited!

Or, one day, your neighbor, who is in the middle of baking, asks you for a measuring cup, which you gladly let her borrow. Time goes by, and you realize the cup should have been returned to you by now. You have several other measuring cups, so you don't need it. But, still, you complain and say, "It's the principle of the thing!"

We've all been there a time or two. One day God spoke to me as I was trying to make a point while stating, "But it's the principal of the thing." He immediately said, ***"I*** **am the** ***principle*** of ***your everything."*** I never forgot that.

The definition of *principle* is "a rule or standard of personal behavior." God was saying that *He* is the standard when it comes to my behavior. *He* is the standard when it comes to making decisions. *He* is the standard when it comes to reacting to something or someone. We need to ask ourselves, *What would Jesus do or what would Jesus say?* Every decision should point to Jesus; every thought should point to Jesus.

There is a song about Jesus being in the center of our lives—how everything revolves around Him and how nothing in this world will satisfy like Him because He is the only thing that matters. This is all very true.

In Acts 17:23 we read that Paul was in Athens and took notice of their massive idolatry. There was even a statue in the middle of the city which read: To the Unknown God. Before that, in verse 16, it is stated that *[Paul's] spirit was stirred in him (brackets mine).* The word *stirred* is translated "provoked to anger, urge, exasperate." Paul was upset, and he did something about it. He disputed with the people in the synagogues. They accused Paul of worshipping a strange god because he spoke of Jesus and His resurrection (see vv. 17-18). Imagine Jesus being a strange god! Paul spoke to the crowd and told them if they would seek God they would find Him because He wasn't far from them (see v. 27).

Then in verse 28, Paul states: *For in him we live, and move, and have our being.* Studying the original Greek meaning of these words gives us a clearer understanding of what this verse really is saying.

In him we live... The Greek word for *live* is *zao*, which means "fresh, strong, efficient, and powerful; to have true life and worthy of the name; to be active, blessed and endless in the kingdom of God; of morals or character." Living in Him simply means how we conduct our lives; how we behave—our thoughts, words, and lifestyle or daily routine. We should live our lives strong, efficiently, powerfully, and blessed!

and move... The Greek word for *move* is *kineo*, which means "to move, set in motion; excite, disturb, throw into commotion and to stir." As Christians, we are to create a stir! But not in order to intentionally bring division. If we truly live as Christ intended, and not follow the ways of the world, then we will seem peculiar to unbelievers—as well as, sad to say, some of the church world.

In Mark 16:17-18 Jesus said,

> *And these signs shall follow them that believe; In my name shall they cast out devils; they shall speak with new tongues; They shall take up serpents; and if they drink any deadly thing, it shall not hurt them; they shall lay hands on the sick, and they shall recover.*

Personally, I believe the Word when it says that I am able to cast out devils and that I can speak in new tongues. I believe that I am protected, and I believe if I lay my hands on the sick, they shall recover! And it's all Jesus doing it through me. Hallelujah!

But I also know that believing this way can cause no small stir in the world as well as in some of the church community. Nonetheless, we should *move* as the Word says to move.

and have our being... The Greek word for *being* is *semen*, which means "who we are, to have hope, have our being." There should be an inner contentment among Christians from knowing who we are in Christ. It should bring us great peace no matter what we may be going through. Paul was saying we are IN Christ! The very Godhead dwells within us; this is who we are. And we have hope as we allow Jesus to conform us into the image of His Son.

If we live and move and have our being in Jesus, then He would be the center of our lives; He would be the principle of our everything. But it's up to *us* to keep Jesus in the center of everything. To pray and ask Jesus to be the center of our lives would be an incorrect prayer because Jesus made Himself available 2,000 years ago when He died on the cross. But as to whether we allow Him to live as the center of our lives is totally up to us.

I recently heard a man tell of a time when God spoke to him, saying, "You have My undivided attention." This immediately made me think of a dog we had named Louie. Louie loved his master, which was my husband. The dog followed Al wherever he went. Whenever I looked outside and Al was on his tractor, the dog followed. Louie was relaying a message to Al: "You have my undivided attention; don't you realize that? I am paying 100 percent attention to you. I see your every move; I want to be by your side always; I want to enjoy the backyard with you; I want to enjoy a car ride with you. Don't you notice me?"

This is a picture of our heavenly Father with us. He is constantly paying attention to us. His eyes are on us all the time. He waits for us to acknowledge Him in *all* of our ways, not just when we need Him desperately.

A bit of an extreme, yet profound example of living and moving and having our being in Him came across my mind recently. Our daughter was married last year, which involved much planning, as you can imagine. As we were planning the reception, I thought it would be wonderful to have a prayer with everyone during the moments right before the dinner. That thought led to possibly playing a worship song following the prayer and having everyone sing along. Then I saw myself and other Christians coming to the front to ask if anyone needed prayer. Then I imagined people coming forth, being prayed for, and getting healed! Suddenly, I was turning my daughter's wedding reception into a healing service! A bit much? Yes.

Here's why my thoughts went that way: I am saturated with God, and I live and move and have my being in Him. Because I have allowed everything in my life to revolve around Jesus, my thoughts naturally went in that direction.

I challenge you today to make Jesus the principle of your everything. It's never too late. Make a decision today to look to Him FIRST for every decision, every thought you have, every word you speak, every action you take, and every reaction. He will never let you down!

Chapter Eight

May I?

For this purpose the Son of God was manifested, that he might destroy the works of the devil.

1 John 3:8

Thinking back on my childhood, I can remember a game we used to play called "Mother, May I?" One child, playing the mother, stood at one side of the room, while the rest of the children stood at the opposite side. One of the children would ask the mother something like, "Mother, may I take three steps forward?" The mother would either give permission or say no depending on what she felt like at the moment. The goal was to be the first one to reach the mother. Whoever did that would become the mother for the next round of play.

In the spiritual realm, the concept of permission has three main facets: (1) The devil needs our permission to act in our lives; (2) we must give God permission to act in our lives; and (3) we need permission from ourselves to see results in our lives.

The devil needs our permission to act in our lives.

Scripture is clear in telling us that the devil is a crushed and defeated foe.

> *That through death he [Jesus] might destroy him that had the power of death, that is, the devil. Hebrews 2:14 (brackets mine)*

The Greek meaning of the word *destroy* is "unemployed; inactivate; to render idle; having no further efficiency; to deprive of force, influence and power; to cause to cease; put an end to; do away with; abolish; annul; to declare invalid (when marriages get annulled it means it's as if they never took place); to pass away; to be severed; separated; discharged; loosed from; to terminate all intercourse with one."

Clearly, the devil's work is destroyed! The whole purpose of Jesus coming to earth was so He would destroy the works of the devil.

For this purpose the Son of God was manifested, that He might destroy the works of the devil. 1 John 3:8

Destroy here means to "dissolve, dismiss, undo, annul, do away with, to deprive of authority, to declare unlawful, break up, demolish, destroy, overthrow."

The devil is defeated; his works are destroyed because of the cross. But if this is true, why are so many Christians suffering at the hands of the enemy? If he is powerless and defeated, then how can he possibly bring destruction to people? We see a lot of this in the body of Christ. There are churches full of sick, defeated, broke, poor, and miserable people who never miss a Sunday service!

The answer is because we give him permission to enter. The devil can't do anything to us that we don't allow. I know a lot of people don't like this because most people don't like to take responsibility for what actually happens in their lives, but it's true. Without realizing it we open the door up for the enemy to come in.

First Peter 5:8 tells us to *Be sober, be vigilant; because your adversary the devil, as a roaring lion, walketh about, seeking whom he may devour. Devour* means "to destroy or swallow up."

Satan is *not* a roaring lion, but he acts *as* a roaring lion. He wants to scare you; he wants you to think he is big and strong and that you should be afraid of him, just like we would fear a real lion. But in actuality, all he can do is roar; he's just a loud mouth. It's either through intimidation or ignorance that Christians let the devil destroy them.

Notice the word *may* in this verse. *The devil seeks whom he may devour.* In other words, he is asking permission: "May I enter in?" And sad to say, many times, we say yes.

One day Al was sitting on the back porch. He noticed a tiny hole in the corner of the screen. In Florida, you don't want to give any creature, such as a lizard, gecko, or snake an opportunity to enter. The Lord spoke to Al through this situation and said that all the devil needs is a tiny opening to enter into the lives of Christians. So small that it could go unnoticed. This little hole is called "permission." One of the ways we give him permission is through strife.

For where envying and strife is, there is confusion and every evil work. James 3:16

This verse tells us that *every* evil work comes from envying and strife! People either don't know this scripture exists, or they don't believe that strife opens up a big door to the devil. Living in strife is giving the devil permission into your life.

We could be believing for our healing, but it would be to no avail if we are in strife. Where there is strife there is confusion. We know from 1 Corinthians 14:33 that God is not the author of confusion, so wherever there is envy and strife, the devil is present.

Years ago we ministered to a couple who lost a son to a disease. It was difficult to minister to the parents because we knew that God wasn't the one who took that child's life. It's hard to come to terms with the truth that somewhere, someone, other than God, messed up. The devil got in their lives somewhere because there was a hole in the "screen."

Several weeks had passed, and this very distraught couple called us. They said they realized why their son died. It was because of strife within the family. They saw the open door the devil had every time there was an argument or disagreement with other members of their family.

There's a lot of emotion when a child is sick, and I'm sure there were many times the family members disagreed on treatment or other issues having to do with this situation. But they realized this presented a huge opportunity for the devil to enter in, and they lost their son.

When we are in strife, there is confusion; but when we are in peace we can hear clearly from God who will show us the necessary steps to healing. They saw that, because of a lack of peace, they couldn't hear clearly. Their child did not die from the disease itself, but from the results of the medication administered to him during that time. But I marveled that they were willing to come to terms with the fact that they may have had something to do with his death.

I also had a family member who had a sick little girl. The family member said to me, "If she doesn't make it, then I will know beyond a shadow of a doubt that it wasn't God; somehow, I missed something. And I can live with that because I have to." She had knowledge and strength. That little girl is with Jesus today.

We are the ones that give the enemy permission to create havoc in our lives, and strife is one way we give him permission. The devil starts talking to us, saying things like, "How could you let that person get away with what he just said to you?" This is his way of asking, "May I enter into your life?"

And we say yes by responding, "Yeah, who does he think he is talking to me like that?" We then confront the person who offended us, the strife begins, and the devil enters. He now has permission to create havoc in our lives.

While James 3:16 reveals what happens when we invite strife, the next verse discusses the opposite of strife:

> *But the wisdom that is from above is first pure, then peaceable, gentle and easy to be intreated, full of mercy and good fruits, without partiality, and without hypocrisy. (v. 17)*

We need to, on purpose, walk away from any opportunity to be in strife. It's hard on the flesh to not engage in strife, but the outcome is well worth it.

Of course, strife is not the only way we give the devil permission to enter; he can also come into our lives through unforgiveness because of an offense, by us giving in to temptation to sin, or various other ways. Regardless, the devil can only get involved if we give him permission.

We must give God permission to act in our lives.

People get turned off by this concept because they see it as arrogance that we could ever take the position of being in charge of God, like we are His boss and what we say goes. It is true that our words are important and that we will have what we say, but this does not mean that we are in charge of God. We use our words to bring into manifestation what God has already ordained for us. When we become born again or get saved, we immediately give Jesus permission to come and reside inside of us.

> *I am the door: by me if any man enter in, he shall be saved, and shall go in and out, and find pasture. The thief cometh not, but for to steal, and to kill, and to destroy: I am come that they might have life, and that they might have it more abundantly. John 10:9-10*

The Lord is asking permission to come and reside in us. When we say yes, we give Him permission to do so; thus, giving us abundant life. Jesus will not force Himself on anyone; He is a gentleman, so He asks permission. It's up to us whether we say yes or no, just like it's up to the mother when playing "Mother, May I?"

Another way we give God permission can be found in 1 Peter 5:6: *Humble yourselves therefore under the mighty hand of God, that He* ***may*** *exalt you in due time (emphasis mine).*

Here, Peter says that God *may* exalt us in due time. God wants to exalt us; He wants us to prosper. He wants to promote us, so He will ask for permission to do so. We can give Him that permission by being humble.

We learned in Chapter 5 that humbling ourselves is two-fold. It involves casting our care onto the Lord (1 Peter 5:7) and actively fighting against the devil (1 Peter 5:8). Humility is two-fold. We must cast our care, but we also must fight the devil with the Word of God. We should not ignore the problem but face it head on with the Word—God's promises. When done correctly, when we are humble by casting our care and fighting, we give God permission to exalt us, to promote us, to fix the problem, and to make sure we end up on top!

We need permission from ourselves to see results in our lives.

God has already done everything when He sent Jesus to the cross. Once He died and rose again and we accepted that, we were born again and were given *all* that Jesus is. When we received Jesus and we believed, we received it all. There's nothing more we need to receive; we now need to learn how to release what we have received.

I think it's important to make this clear because I often hear that we need to learn how to receive. I understand what people mean when they say this, but we need to be careful how we use our words. We can't receive what we have already received, but we can release it so we can see the manifestation in our lives.

The Word is *release* and we do it by *faith*. It comes from the *inside out!* We have to know that we have a choice as to what we will release. We can either release good or bad. We can either release from our inner Spirit man, or we release something from our mind, will, emotions, or soul.

Unfortunately there are times when we give ourselves permission to do things we ought to think twice about. We permit ourselves to listen to certain music that does not edify; we permit ourselves to watch certain TV programs or movies that do not build us up but tear us down; and we permit ourselves to become offended, to become angry, and to speak and act in ways that the Bible teaches against.

I can permit myself to be afraid of the future; I can give myself permission to take something that doesn't belong to me. I can give myself permission to become offended. We must change this. Instead, we have to permit ourselves to release all that's in our Spirit man. But it's our choice what we will permit. We are always permitting something, so it might as well be something good.

We have authority. Will we permit ourselves to use it? We have mercy. Will we permit ourselves to extend it to others? We have boldness. Will we permit ourselves to boldly proclaim truth? We have kindness. Will we permit ourselves to treat others kindly? We have joy. Will we permit ourselves to rejoice in the Lord always? We have peace. Will we permit ourselves to walk in that peace and refrain from strife?

The ball is in our court. A minister once said that God is up there doing a whole lot of nothing because He did it all at the cross. It's now up to us. It's our choice as to what we permit to be released in our lives.

I'd like to conclude this chapter with a true family story that serves as a great example of this principle. My niece was recently pregnant with her second child. She works in an ultrasound lab, and several months into her pregnancy she had an ultrasound taken by one of her friends in the office. The test showed an abnormality in the lateral ventricles of the baby's brain. The baby's brain and kidneys appeared slightly dilated. This could cause water on the brain, creating pressure, which could possibly lead to seizures. This scared both my niece and her friend. They both knew what they were looking at, and it wasn't good. They've seen this situation many times with their past patients.

My niece texted me and asked for prayer. I prayed for the baby for about a month. Then, one day, my niece was very strong on my heart, so I spent hours praying for the baby. I prayed mostly in tongues because I didn't know exactly how to pray in English.

The Lord then led me to tell her that He wants her to ignore those test results and pretend that they never existed, and that if there is another ultrasound that appears the same to just disregard it because the baby is healed! She was to just believe it regardless of what the tests say. She thanked me and began to believe what the Word said about her situation. One week later, unbeknownst to me, she had another ultrasound and then gave me a praise report.

The lateral ventricles were both showing as normal. Apparently, the baby just has a big head! But here's the key: When I told her what God said, she did what God said to do. She gave herself permission to believe the Word rather than what she saw in the natural.

We may conclude that the baby never had that problem in the first place, but as far as my niece and her friend were concerned, it looked like the baby had a problem. If she fell apart from fear and spoke fear and believed the report (releasing the negative), then the devil would have had permission to come in and actually create this problem. But because she chose to believe the Word of the Lord (releasing life), she shut the devil out, which resulted in the baby just having a big head.

It's possible that the baby could have had a problem in the first place, and God healed the baby because my niece believed it and released health and life. Either way, we had the victory, and the baby was born perfectly normal; so normal, in fact, the doctors didn't even think of running a test "just in case."

So when you hear the question, "May I?" remember, if it is coming from your inner Spirit man, then answer with a resounding yes!

Chapter Nine

Rewards in Heaven

For the Son of man shall come in the glory of his Father with his angels; and then he shall reward every man according to his works.

Matthew 16:27

In speaking with many Christians over the years, I've found most believe that when they die they will stand before Jesus, at which point He will make the determination of whether they will go to heaven or hell for eternity. They believe that Jesus will review their lives on earth, and if He is dissatisfied with what He sees He will send them to hell; if He is pleased He lets them into heaven. There are certain denominations that believe if you don't confess ALL of the sins you've committed throughout your life, or if one sin is left out because you forgot to ask for forgiveness, God sends you to hell.

I began to realize that this is why so many people are afraid to die—they aren't really sure what will happen to them afterward. They're not *really* sure where they'll spend eternity. This would be a terrible feeling, especially if you are elderly and sick and you see your life coming to an end.

I knew a woman who never served God during her entire life. She was eighty-six years old when she had a stroke, which left her bedridden for the next two years. Shortly after the stroke, it seemed that she was in her right mind for a short while, so I asked her if she wanted to become a Christian. She said yes; she was ready. Praise the Lord! She repeated the prayer after me and was saved.

Unfortunately, she was never able to experience the love of God in her daily life because she was so sick for those two years. She also did not get to fulfill God's plan for her in this life. It was obvious during her last two years that she was striving to stay alive. Minutes before she went to be with Jesus, she was physically out of control trying not to die. Her arms and legs were swinging wildly, pushing herself out of bed. She was working very hard at running away from death. She could no longer fight, and her body just gave up. It was very sad.

She fought so hard because she was truly scared. She never learned about what really happens when you accept Jesus, and she was unsure of what God would do with her when she stood before Him. What a horrible way to die.

Many years ago I had a dream that I was in my bedroom sitting on a chair, and something very strange came over me physically. It was so weird that I was certain this was my time and I was going to die. It wasn't something I just guessed; I knew it. But how did I feel? Completely peaceful. There was no fear anywhere in me; not even a touch of it!

There was another incident that was not a dream. My husband and I were on an airplane flying into LaGuardia Airport in New York. LaGuardia has a very short runway, which I didn't know about at that time. I was in the window seat, and as we were landing, I noticed that the plane was just above the water. It didn't look right; we were too close to the water. I thought those were going to be the last moments of my life. I thought for sure we would crash in the water, as I saw no land in sight.

About two seconds before we landed, the runway suddenly appeared, and we touched ground. Although I thought for sure I was going to die, I was at total peace. I grabbed my husband's hand and remained quiet.

Why did I have this reaction? Because I knew that in mere seconds I would be with Jesus! How could I be so sure? I was assured. Assurance simply means freedom from doubt. I have a confident realization in the finished work of Jesus Christ for me, personally. Even though sometimes I feel like it and sometimes I don't, it doesn't change the truth that I am personally secure in Christ.

This is because my salvation had nothing to do with me and everything to do with Jesus. If it had anything to do with my performance, my salvation wouldn't last because not long after my conversion I would sin and lose my salvation. It can't depend on my performance, and thank God it doesn't because I would fail every time! Thank God my salvation is secure based on what Jesus did on the cross and not on anything that I may have done.

I admit there were times early on in my walk with the Lord when I questioned my salvation. But it was only because I did something that wasn't right; I sinned. I felt guilty because I had lived under a Law-based performance mentality for so long. But today as I walk with the Lord and see His amazing love for me, and as I learn that He knows my heart even when I mess up and even when my own heart condemns me (see 1 John 3:20), it creates in me a strong confidence. The Word says that when our heart condemns us, He is greater than our heart (see 1 John 3:20). He knows the truth about our right position with Him even when we may question it (see 1 John 3:21). This causes my confidence in the Word to grow.

> *For by grace ye are saved through faith; and that not of yourselves: it is the gift of God, not of works, lest any man should boast. Ephesians 2:8-9*

If the Bible says I'm saved by His grace, then I'm saved by His grace! That settles it. I have confidence in that!

Where we spend eternity is decided now while we are on the earth; not when we stand before Jesus after we've died. And *we* are the ones who decide; not God.

The following passages instruct us to believe. Jesus made it possible for everyone who was ever born to be saved. Our part is simply to believe. When we believe something we embrace it.

For I am not ashamed of the gospel of Christ: for it is the power of God unto salvation to every one that ***believeth****; to the Jew first, and also to the Greek. Romans 1:16 (emphasis mine)*

Even the righteousness of God which is by faith of Jesus Christ unto all and upon all them that ***believe****: for there is no difference. Romans 3:22 (emphasis mine)*

But to him that worketh not, but ***believeth*** *on him that justifieth the ungodly, his faith is counted for righteousness. Romans 4:5 (emphasis mine)*

There may be questions that arise after we choose to believe, but as we walk with the Lord and educate ourselves in His Word we become more assured of the fact that we will be in heaven someday with Jesus! Full assurance brings peace. Having assurance like this removes the fear of punishment or of dying.

But many people want to know about Christ's judgment, due to scriptures such as the following:

For we shall all stand before the judgment seat of Christ. Romans 14:10

For we must all appear before the judgment seat of Christ; that every one may receive the things done in his body, according to that he hath done, whether it be good or bad. 2 Corinthians 5:10

We will not be judged as to whether we are saved; remember, that's already been decided by us. The judgment we will receive is the judgment of rewards. Often people will confuse the difference between salvation and rewards. Salvation is a gift, but rewards are earned by our works *after* we are saved. Salvation is a present reality, but our rewards will be given in the future, in heaven.

This is explained in 1 Corinthians 3:5-15.

Who then is Paul, and who is Apollos, but ministers by whom ye believed, even as the Lord gave to every man? I have planted, Apollos watered; but God gave the increase. So then neither is he that planteth any thing, neither he that watereth; but God that giveth the increase. Now he that planteth and he that watereth are one: and every man shall receive his own reward according to his own labour. [Referring to working for the Lord and receiving a reward.] For we are labourers together with God: ye are God's husbandry, ye are God's building. According to the grace of God which is given unto me, as a wise masterbuilder, I have laid the foundation, and another buildeth thereon. But let every man take heed how he buildeth thereupon. For other foundation can no man lay than that is laid, which is Jesus Christ. Now if any man build upon this foundation gold, silver, precious stones, wood, hay, stubble; Every man's work shall be made manifest: for the day shall declare it, because it shall be revealed by fire; and the fire shall try every man's work of what sort it is. If any man's work abide which he hath built thereupon, he shall receive a reward. If any man's work shall be burned, he shall suffer loss: but he himself shall be saved; yet so as by fire. (brackets mine)

God will test our works by the fire of motive. If we did things in His strength and for His glory, they will pass through the refining fire and emerge as gold, silver, and costly stones. If we did things in our own flesh and for our own glory, then those works will be burned up and will not make it through the testing fire. These works of the flesh are referred to as wood, hay, and stubble, which are easily consumed by flames.

Looking again at verse 13:

> *Every man's work shall be made manifest: for the day shall declare it, because it shall be revealed by fire; and the fire shall try every man's work of* ***what sort it is.*** *(emphasis mine)*

We can be misled into thinking that if our ministry is not big, then it doesn't count with God, or maybe we'll get fewer rewards than those who are preaching to millions. That's not so. As long as you are doing what God told you to do you will receive the same reward as those whom God told to preach to millions of people! It's not the size of our ministry; it's the obedience to what God has called us to do. The question we need to ask ourselves is: Are we doing what God said to do?

When my husband and I left our church at the Lord's leading, it seemed like nothing happened for a while. We just continued to learn about God's Word on our own. We see now how that was exactly what God wanted us to do during that time. Isn't that great? Just sitting around learning produced gold, silver, and costly stones! Why? Because God told us to do that.

Then people started calling us and showing up at our front door. These people needed answers. Their lives were a mess. So we ministered for years to people one on one. Although no one knew who we were, and we did not have a big pulpit ministry like others, we knew we were doing exactly what God wanted us to do. At times, it really didn't look like we were doing much for the Lord, but Jesus is interested in the individual. If we can help one person turn his or her life around, that's all that's important. One-on-one ministry, if that's what God calls you to do, is as reward-able as a Billy Graham ministry! Don't ever judge your ministry by its size!

Our works will be revealed on Judgment Day as to whether they are of our own doing or led by the Lord. We will be rewarded if they were Spirit led, and we will suffer loss if they were fleshly.

How can we tell the difference? Did God tell you to do what you are doing, or is it your own idea? Or, did God give you the plan, but then you took it from there and never included Him in any decisions after the initial direction? What we did on this earth must be in agreement with God's plan for our lives; if not, we will suffer loss.

Again, this has nothing to do with our salvation. Verse 15 says *but he himself shall be saved*—even though he suffers loss. Our salvation is secure; the judgment is for rewards! God is so good. How can there be any fear of dying once we know this?

The following scriptures speak about rewards:

> *Rejoice and be exceedingly glad: for great is your reward in heaven. Matthew 5:12*

> *He that receiveth a prophet in the name of a prophet shall receive a prophet's reward; and he that receiveth a righteous man in the name of a righteous man shall receive a righteous man's reward. Matthew 10:41*

> *For the Son of man shall come in the glory of his Father with his angels; and then he shall reward every man according to his works. Matthew 16:27*

For whosoever shall give you a cup of water to drink in my name, because ye belong to Christ, verily I say unto you, he shall not lose his reward. Mark 9:41

Rejoice ye in that day, and leap for joy: for, behold, your reward is great in heaven: for in the like manner did their fathers unto the prophets. Luke 6:23

If any man's work abide which he hath built thereupon, he shall receive a reward. 1 Corinthians 3:14

In addition to our rewards, the Bible discusses believers receiving five different crowns. I believe these are real crowns we receive, but there are some who think they are spoken of figuratively. Either way, we will be receiving from the Lord! Let's look at them briefly:

The Incorruptible Crown

And every man that striveth for the mastery is temperate in all things. Now they do it to obtain a corruptible crown; but we an incorruptible. 1 Corinthians 9:25

Paul talked about running a race. Paul ran his race to win. He went all the way for the kingdom of God. He was comparing receiving an earthly crown with an incorruptible crown. Paul said in Verse 24 to *run that ye may obtain. Obtain* means "to seize eagerly that which you have your eyes and your heart set upon." We should live the Christian life as the greatest opportunity that we've ever had, taking every opportunity with great excitement and eagerness.

The Crown of Righteousness

> *Henceforth there is laid up for me a crown of righteousness, which the Lord, the righteous judge, shall give me at that day: and not to me only, but unto all them also that love his appearing. 2 Timothy 4:8*

If we know that we have been made righteous by what Jesus has done and not by our own efforts, and if we love God and look forward to His return, then this crown is for us!

The Crown of Glory

> *And when the chief Shepherd shall appear, ye shall receive a crown of glory that fadeth not away. 1 Peter 5:4*

This passage speaks about those who are mature in the Lord teaching others. We, as ministers, are to be willing to minister gently and patiently. We are to have right motives and not be in it for the money, not being lords over others but examples to them. If we do it this way, then we are promised the crown of glory!

The Crown of Rejoicing

> *For what is our hope, or joy, or crown of rejoicing? Are not even ye in the presence of our Lord Jesus Christ at his coming? 1 Thessalonians 2:19*

We will receive this crown by leading people to Jesus and/or by disciplining them to become mature in the Lord. Paul was telling his converts that *they* were his joy; those we minister to should be our joy too.

The Crown of Life

> *Fear none of those things which thou shalt suffer: behold, the devil shall cast some of you into prison, that ye may be tried; and ye shall have tribulation ten days: be thou faithful unto death, and I will give thee a crown of life. Revelation 2:10*

This crown is for those who remain faithful in the midst of trials and persecution. Many just quit and give up on their faith because they don't see things working fast enough.

No matter how hard it may be, if we stand faithful to God's Word, sometimes even to the point of death, we will receive this crown.

This was just a quick overview of the crowns listed in Scripture. I do not believe our rewards are limited to these five crowns. Our God is limitless. We probably will be given rewards for things we can't even think of! It's a time to look forward to.

There's also the question of our position in heaven. When someone has a crown, that person is also in a position of authority. I believe there may be different positions in heaven based on the rewards we receive. We are not going to get rewards just for the sake of getting them. They have to benefit us in some way. I believe this benefit will be found in the positions of authority. I don't think heaven is just a bunch of clouds, and we float from one cloud to another all day. I believe it will be a full society with people holding different positions of authority, which will be based on what they did on earth for the Lord.

This all comes back to where we began. If there were no rewards in heaven, then why do anything for the Lord?

God wants us to fulfill His plan here on the earth so He can reward us fully on that great and glorious day!

Chapter Ten

So, What's the Difference?

For if that first covenant had been faultless, then should no place have been sought for the second.

Hebrews 8:7

Understanding the difference between the Old Testament and the New Testament is crucial in the life of a Christian. The Old Testament represents the old covenant that God ordained with man based on laws that people had to obey to avoid God's judgment. God had no choice but to put these laws into effect because of the immeasurable acts of sin and disobedience in the land.

Of course no one could keep the Law, which was what God wanted to prove to them. Some were able to keep one part of the Law but then failed in another. James 2:10 tells us that if we keep the whole Law but offend in one point we are guilty of all. Understanding that it is impossible to keep the entire Law should lead us to the realization that we need a Savior.

The Old Testament Law did what it was supposed to do. It created frustration in people for not being able to obey all of it. But thank God the Law was only temporary until Jesus came on the scene. Now, we no longer are justified by the Law but by faith in Jesus and what He accomplished on the cross.

> *Wherefore the law was our schoolmaster to bring us unto Christ, that we might be justified by faith. But after that faith is come, we are no longer under a schoolmaster. Galatians 3:24-25*

There is safety in following laws, so the first covenant wasn't wrong; it just was incomplete, revealing the problem but no remedy. The answer was to come. His name is Jesus. Today we are under a much better covenant.

> *But now hath he obtained a more excellent ministry, by how much also he is the mediator of a better covenant, which was established upon better promises. For if that first covenant had been faultless, then*

should no place have been sought for the second. Hebrews 8:6-7

So, what's the difference between the covenants?

For this is the covenant that I will make with the house of Israel after those days, saith the Lord; I will put my laws into their mind, and write them in their hearts: and I will be to them a God, and they shall be to me a people: And they shall not teach every man his neighbour, and every man his brother, saying, Know the Lord: for all shall know me, from the least to the greatest. For I will be merciful to their unrighteousness, and their sins and their iniquities will I remember no more. Hebrews 8:10-12

This passage tells us that in the new covenant the Lord will put His laws into our mind and heart, and we will not have to learn from our neighbor because we will all know God intimately. He will be merciful to our unrighteousness and sins, and He will no longer remember our iniquities.

Because of Jesus we are no longer judged. He came to free us from the curse of the Law (see Gal. 3:13). Jesus was made the curse for us; He took our punishment. God doesn't hold our sins against us any longer. We are now living under the new covenant of grace and mercy; no more guilt and condemnation.

The old covenant was based on *our* holiness; the new covenant is based on His holiness. It's not what *we* do; it's what *He* did. We no longer have to strive to be loved and accepted by God. He took our sins and made us right before Him. Now we can have intimate fellowship with Him because He lives inside of us!

However, just because we are New Testament believers, it doesn't mean that we can't learn from the Old Testament. There is much we can learn as long as we are properly discerning the Word of God as we read it.

In Psalm 51:9-11, David said, *Hide thy face from my sins, and blot out all my iniquities. Create in me a clean heart, O God; and renew a right spirit within me. Cast me not away from thy presence; and take not thy holy spirit from me.*

In the new covenant, all of our sins are forgiven and forgotten, and God does not hold any one of them against us. To ask Him to blot out our iniquities would be an incorrect way to pray today because He has already done this. He treats us as if we've never sinned because He sees us through his Son, Jesus. And through Jesus we are sinless!

According to the new covenant, once we become born again the Holy Spirit abides inside of us and seals us with Himself.

> *Ye were sealed with the Holy Spirit of promise. Ephesians 1:13b*

To pray that God doesn't take His spirit from us is, once again, an incorrect way to pray. In another example, Hebrews 13:5 assures us that God will never leave us nor forsake us. To ask God to not cast us away from His presence is a wrong way to pray.

Although we are no longer living under old covenant principles, there are many Old Testament stories however, that can and should be applied to today's New Testament church.

> *For whatsoever things were written aforetime were written for our learning, that we through patience and comfort of the scriptures might have hope. Romans 15:4*

One such story comes from the book of Ezekiel. Ezekiel was a priest called by God to prophecy to the Israelites when they were taken captive by the Babylonians because of their rebellion toward God. Ezekiel was in captivity with them, and God used him to speak judgment to the Jews. Aren't you glad that God no longer treats us as our sins deserve because of what Jesus did for us?

In Ezekiel 36 God turned His heart back to His people and used Ezekiel to prophecy hope and redemption to them. God never wanted to treat them harshly in the first place. He always loved them. Think of how it hurts us as parents to discipline our children.

Then in Chapter 37 God gave Ezekiel a vision where he is carried down into a valley. The valley was full of bones. God was showing Ezekiel that Israel was spiritually dead, and it seemed impossible for them to ever be restored and revived.

And He said unto me, Son of man, can these bones live? (v. 3)

It seems that this question should come from Ezekiel to God, but this was God asking Ezekiel if he thought the bones could live! God was asking him if Israel could be restored. Ezekiel admitted he didn't know but said that God knew.

> *Again he said unto me, prophecy upon these bones, and say unto them, O ye dry bones, hear the word of the* LORD. *(v. 4)*

God told Ezekiel to speak to the dead, dry bones. Have you ever wondered why God just didn't do it Himself? Then he told Ezekiel what to say to the bones. God said He would cause breath to enter into them, and they would live (see v. 5).

God also told Ezekiel to say that He would lay sinews (tissues connecting muscles to bones) on them and add flesh to them to cover their skin. He would put breath into them so they would live, and they would know that He is the Lord (see v. 6).

Ezekiel did as God commanded him:

> *So I prophesied as I was commanded: and as I prophesied, there was a noise, and behold a shaking, and the bones came together, bone to his bone. (v. 7)*

In verse 8 flesh came upon the bones, but there still was no breath in them. Then the Lord told Ezekiel to prophesy to the wind so that breath would come into them and they would live.

The word *live* here is amazing. The original meaning is "to be free from sickness, discouragement, faintness, death, and poverty." It also means "to live prosperously and be restored to health, revived, quickened, refreshed, and restored." This is not just being alive, this is *living!* Living a life full of purpose and meaning—living the abundant life! Ezekiel spoke *real* life to them.

Verse 8 reminds me of a time when I visited New York and needed to take a taxi. I wasn't looking forward to it, as I never liked being in a taxi with a stranger, locked in the back seat with a plastic panel separating me from the driver. But on this occasion, I had no choice. To my delight, however, it was a regular car without a plastic panel.

The driver began to tell me how hard he works, yet after all his years of driving a taxi, he was broke. He said he lives a very "loose" lifestyle and was generally miserable with life. He was just living; just getting by.

I began speaking the Word of God to him. I told him that God had much more for him; a full, abundant life. I spoke real life to him. By the end of the trip he was filled with hope and an excitement to see what God will do for him in his future. God has a much better life for him than what he could even imagine. He wants that man prosperous and healthy and whole in every way, which is *real* living.

Continuing on in verse 10: *the breath came into them, and they lived, and stood up on their feet, an exceeding great army.*

Why didn't God just prophesy to the bones Himself? He could have. But the truth is, those bones would never have come to life if Ezekiel didn't speak the word of the Lord. If God wanted to do it, He would have. It was up to Ezekiel to hear the word then speak it!

It's exactly the same with us today. Our answer to life's problems is the Word of God. If we are fearful we should speak 2 Timothy 1:7 out loud: *For God hath not given [me] the spirit of fear; but of power, and of love, and of a sound mind (brackets mine).*

If we are sick, we should declare: *By his stripes [I am] healed (1 Peter 2:24, brackets mine).*

If we need to make a decision, we can speak Ephesians 1:8: *He [has] abounded toward me in all wisdom (brackets mine).*

Notice that God performed the miracle only after Ezekiel spoke it! We release the grace of God in our lives by speaking the Word in faith over our situation. God waited on Ezekiel, and He is waiting on us to believe His Word and speak it. He already accomplished everything we need on the cross through His grace. Now, by faith, we must access it.

Can you see the importance of learning from these Old Testament stories? Although we now have a much better covenant through the New Testament, we still need the examples and stories from the Old Testament for God's principles to be learned.

Chapter Eleven

Standing on His Promises

For all the promises of God in him are yea, and in him Amen, unto the glory of God by us.

2 Corinthians 1:20

The Bible is filled with promises from God. Some believe there are about 3,000 promises; others think 7,000. However many there are, it is clear that God wants us to live in His promises daily. He wants us to benefit from them; they are all part of living the abundant life. Because there are too many promises to include in this chapter, we'll just look at a couple of them.

The scriptures teach that we are to give to the poor, and there are many promises in the Bible associated with giving to the poor. Paul himself was eager to do it (see Gal. 2:10). Throughout the Word, we see God's heart when it comes to those who are in need, and we are exhorted to help them.

My husband and I receive so much joy when we give to the poor, but joy is just one of the many blessings we receive when we give.

Blessed is he that considereth the poor: the LORD will deliver him in time of trouble. The LORD will preserve him, and keep him alive; and he shall be blessed upon the earth: and thou wilt not deliver him unto the will of his enemies. The LORD will strengthen him upon the bed of languishing: thou wilt make all his bed in his sickness. Psalm 41:1-3

The Hebrew meaning of the word *consider* means "to look at, ponder, have insight, or give attention to." We are not to look down upon or disregard those who are needy. On the contrary, we are to pay attention to them. We do this by examining their needs and then becoming the answer to their problem.

Once we consider the poor and then meet their need, we are eligible to receive God's promises. Our promise is that He will deliver us in times of trouble. He provides "The Great Escape" out of trouble. I like to see it as God kidnapping us to safety! "Escape" is one of the Hebrew meanings of *deliver.*

God will also protect us from all harm, guard us, and watch over us, and keep us alive, which doesn't mean just getting by but rather living a long, prosperous, and healthy life. He promises that we will be happy on this earth, and He will not hand us over to our enemies—other people in this life or the devil himself!

God promises to sustain, support, and uphold us when we are sick. The last part of this promise is that *He wilt make all his bed in his sickness.* The word *make* is very interesting. The original Hebrew meaning is "to overturn, overthrow, turn back, reverse, transform, turned against." Wow! He will reverse our sickness to the point that there will be no effect of it whatsoever. It will be as if it never happened in the first place!

My husband shattered his pelvis a few years ago, and what could have been months and months of healing turned out to be just five weeks with no surgery. It's an amazing story, but we stood on Psalm 41 through the entire time of healing. In fact, from his hospital bed we gave money to a ministry as well as someone we knew who was in need.

We knew by doing this that we were making a statement to the devil that we trusted God with our money no matter what. The Bible teaches that if we can't trust God with our money, which is the least of everything, then we won't be able to trust Him with other, more important things, such as healing.

> *He that is faithful in that which is least is faithful also in much: and he that is unjust in the least is unjust also in much. Luke 16:10*

In this verse, that which is "least" is referring to money. When we gave money while Al was in the hospital, we were not trying to get something from God, like a quick healing, but we were following the principles in His Word. When you do that, His promises come to pass. This principle can be found in 2 Corinthians 1:20.

> *For all the promises of God in him are yea, and in him Amen, unto the glory of God by us.*

Rather than spending a year healing, the process was accelerated, and at five weeks Al was walking. Within just a couple of months it was as if it never happened to him—until this day! That's the God we serve!

Why were we able to stand on the promises of Psalm 41? Because we were in obedience to it. We obeyed by giving to the poor as the Word instructed us; we then had the right to claim those promises to come to pass in our lives.

There is no law that says we have to give to the poor, but it is an expression of God's heart to do so. Preaching the Law would mean that God would curse or judge us for the sin of not giving to the poor. But God does not do this. It's our decision whether or not we give to those in need, but when we do, we position ourselves to see His promises come to pass in our lives.

God wants us to give to the poor for two reasons: His heart of compassion for them, and His desire to pour out His promises onto us! We should always be looking for ways to help those in need. It's Gods heart, and it should be ours too.

Isaiah 58 is yet another scripture with an awesome promise to those who consider the poor. In this passage God was rebuking the Israelites. They were seeking God daily but only for the outward appearance. They fasted for all the wrong reasons, such as a religious routine or for being in competition with one another.

In verses 6 and 7 God told them the type of fast that pleases Him.

> *Is not this the fast that I have chosen? to loose the bands of wickedness, to undo the heavy burdens, and to let the oppressed go free, and that ye break every yoke? Is it not to deal thy bread to the hungry, and that thou bring the poor that are cast out to thy house? when thou seest the naked, that thou cover him; and that thou hide not thyself from thine own flesh?*

God exhorted them to help others. He is telling us the same thing today: to feed others, clothe them, give them shelter, and not to forget our families. This is interesting because there are times we treat others better than our own families. Sometimes we may not even notice a family member is in need because we are so busy meeting the needs of others outside the family. Sometimes we know those in our family all too well, and we tend to judge them more than those we don't know as well. I believe this is why the Lord included the phrase, *and that thou hide not thyself from thine own flesh.*

Here are some promises that we can count on if we do these things:

Then shall thy light break forth as the morning... (v. 8)

The Hebrew meaning of the word *light* is "happiness and prosperity." Have you ever seen a sunrise? It rises quickly. You can almost see it move second by second, and as it rises, it becomes more and more beautiful. And in a second, it's there in its fullness and beauty. God promises that we will have joy and prosperity as quickly and as beautiful as the sunrise!

And thy health shall spring forth speedily: and thy righteousness shall go before thee; the glory of the LORD *shall be thy reward. (v. 8)*

If we are sick we will recover quickly; our right standing with God will be visible to others as we enjoy our salvation, walking in victory, prosperity, justice, and vindication in controversy. Then we are rewarded even more with God's glory, which is His abundance, riches, splendor, honor, dignity, reputation, and reverence!

Verses 10 and 11 continue with even more promises:

And if thou draw out thy soul to the hungry, and satisfy the afflicted soul; then shall thy light rise in obscurity,

> *and thy darkness be as the noon day. And the* LORD *shall guide thee continually, and satisfy thy soul in drought, and make fat thy bones: and thou shalt be like a watered garden, and like a spring of water, whose waters fail not. (vv. 10-11)*

If we feed the hungry, our darkness will be as the noon, and we will be satisfied for all necessities of life.

We can count on God's promises. At times, however, it may look like His promises are not working even though you give to the poor. Why would this be? Because you must receive these promises by faith! You must believe them to be true. They are like any other promise in the Bible. They don't automatically come to pass. They are there for us, but we must receive them by faith.

We must stand on every promise in the Word of God, knowing that they all will come to pass even if we don't see it right away. To *stand* means "to have or maintain a position on an issue or to hold one's ground." This is what we did when Al broke his hip. Those five weeks were dismal and painful, moment by moment. But we stood on these promises, and what should have taken almost a year took just a couple of months. We have a right to these promises because God says so in His Word.

We should expect these promises to come to pass in our lives like when we expect a package in the mail. We inform other family members that we are expecting a package, and they are to look out for it. In the same way that we eagerly await the package we should eagerly await the manifestation of God's promises.

Our motive for helping those in need should never be so His promises will work for us, although it is true that they will. We should give to the poor because we share the heart of God. It was so important to Jesus that we meet the needs of others that He said when we feed or clothe the poor or when we visit the sick or those in prison, we are doing it unto Him (see Matt. 25:40). He is touched that much by people's infirmities. We are His hands and His feet. Let's use them and then see His awesome promises work in our lives.

Chapter Twelve

Switch Your Thinking

Finally my brethren, whatsoever things are true, whatsoever things are honest, whatsoever things are just, whatsoever things are pure, whatsoever things are lovely, whatsoever things are of a good report, if there be any virtue, and if there be any praise, think on these things.

Philippians 4:8

God actually tells us in His Word how we should think. At times thinking like God might be hard to do, but it is possible. He wouldn't tell us to do something that was not possible.

I don't think we realize how important our thoughts are. When things are going well in our lives, we think happy thoughts, but what about when we go through tough times? What do we think on when an unexpected trial forces its way into our lives? The way we choose to think is the way the course of that particular situation will go. It's crucial that our thoughts line up with the Word of God at the onset of any trial. It's possible to do this, and it will turn any situation around.

> *Now before the feast of the passover, when Jesus knew that his hour was come that he should depart out of this world unto the Father, having loved his own which were in the world, he loved them unto the end. And supper being ended, the devil having now put into the heart of Judas Iscariot, Simon's son, to betray him; Jesus knowing that the Father had given all things into his hands, and that he was come from God, and went to God; He riseth from supper, and laid aside his garments; and took a towel, and girded himself. After that he poureth water into a bason, and began to wash the disciples' feet, and to wipe them with the towel wherewith he was girded. John 13:1-5*

In verse 1 Jesus began to think on three things: (1) His hour had come; (2) He would be leaving this world; and (3) He would be going to His Father. He started thinking of what was coming, and He knew it wouldn't be pretty. I believe this was an opportunity for Jesus to become fearful. Hebrews 4:15 says that in all points He was tempted as we are.

Jesus came to earth both fully divine and fully human… the Son of God and Son of man. Yet He chose to set His divinity aside and operate solely in His humanity so He could be like you and me! He set aside all the glory and honor that came with being King, and although He had all the attributes of God, He chose not to benefit from any one of them.

This is what Jesus was trying to show His disciples; that He was human just like they were. And if they depended on the Holy Spirit like He did, they could do the same things He did! This is still for us today. As He was thinking of what was about to happen, I'm sure He was tempted with fear.

In verse 1 Jesus' thoughts turned to His disciples. He loved them dearly, unto the end, which simply means forever. He was protective of them, and He was concerned for them because He knew they weren't strong in their faith. He knew they would despair and desert Him because of fear; they would not take it well.

I believe Jesus was tempted to become worried about them. A good example would be a mom who has just been diagnosed with a fatal disease and is told she only has two years to live. What is the first thing she thinks of? Her children, of course. She would become concerned over their welfare: *How would they handle not having a mom? Who would take care of them? Should she tell them?* All of these thoughts would naturally come into her mind. I believe Jesus may have experienced some of those same feelings toward His disciples.

In verse 2 supper has ended, and Jesus knew He was getting even closer to the inevitable. He began to think of the one who would betray Him. Verse 11 tells us that Jesus knew whom His betrayer was:

> *For he knew who should betray him; therefore said he, Ye are not all clean.*

How do you suppose Jesus knew who would betray Him? How could He know all of these things if He operated in His humanity? I believe there are three reasons.

First, He was intimate with His Father. He only spoke

what He heard the Father speak (see John 8:26), and He only did what the Father told Him to do (see John 8:28). He was connected as *one* with His Father. We need to ask ourselves if we are connected to the Father as Jesus was. Second, Jesus knew the scriptures and all that was prophesied about Him (see Isa. 53, for example). And third, Jesus operated in the gifts of the Holy Spirit—the word of wisdom, word of knowledge, gift of prophecy, gift of faith, gift of healing, working of miracles, and the discerning of spirits. We, too, should operate in the gifts of the Spirit if we want the same results as Jesus had.

As I was reading these scriptures, I noticed something about Jesus. He may have thought things contrary to what His Father thought, but He never spoke them out of His mouth! This is important. It's one thing for the thought to come into our minds, but it's quite another to speak it out loud. If we allow negative thoughts to linger, they will eventually come out of our mouths, which will make our situation worse. We will have what we say!

In Verse 3 Jesus continued to think, but something changes. Up until this point His thoughts were progressively going downhill. But verse 3 is where Jesus makes the change.

He remembered something. He reminded Himself of who He was in His Father and that His Father had given all things into His hands, such as power and authority, which He could use at anytime.

He also reminded Himself of where He came from and where He was going. Jesus *changed His thinking!* We know that if He continued to think as He had been, it would have brought great fear and despair on Him, as it would to any of us. So, *on purpose,* He changed what He was thinking.

What exactly did that do for Him? It gave Him the strength to continue to do what He was called to do, and that was to be a servant. He began to wash His disciples' feet, including the feet of His betrayer, Judas. It also gave Him the strength to endure great affliction for us.

But Jesus also knew the end. Both verses 1 and 3 tell us that He knew He was going back to the Father. He knew what would be accomplished by going to the cross, and this also strengthened Him. Hebrews 12:2 tells us: *Who for the joy that was set before him endured the cross.*

This is like having a baby. The woman knows that she may experience great pain in delivering her child and maybe even experience an uncomfortable few months leading up to the delivery, but she is willing to endure the pain because of the joy of having her own child. The joy Jesus had was knowing that we would all be invited into His Kingdom because of the cross. He would have many children!

When we go through trials, we too must remind ourselves of some things. Some of the issues can be enormous, but this is why we need to, *on purpose*, align our thoughts with the Word of God; and the sooner the better.

If there is an opportunity in my life to become fearful over something I just heard, I immediately go into a private area and begin speaking the Word of God over the situation, taking my authority over all the plans of the evil one. I do this until I feel confident and assured. We can't just get rid of bad thoughts and leave it at that. We must replace them with good thoughts. If not, then the negative thoughts will remain and grow until there is so much fear we give in to the battle. It's a fight to keep our thoughts in line with God's Word, but it's worth it.

Rather than focusing on the problem and talking about the problem and trying to fix the problem, we should be reminding ourselves of who we are in Christ and what we have in Him, and then begin using our power and authority. This is when we become unstoppable. No devil in hell can fight that because we know all things are under our feet (see Eph. 1:22). The victory is ours! Amen!

Chapter Thirteen

Take Authority Now!

For verily I say unto you, That whosoever shall say unto this mountain, Be thou removed, and be thou cast into the sea; and shall not doubt in his heart, but shall believe that those things which he saith shall come to pass; he shall have whatsoever he saith.

Mark 11:23

We know from Scripture that God has given us His authority. It began with Adam and Eve in the Garden of Eden. God gave them dominion over all the earth.

And God blessed them, and God said unto them, Be fruitful, and multiply, and replenish the earth, and subdue it: and have dominion over the fish of the sea, and over the fowl of the air, and over every living thing that moveth upon the earth. And God said, Behold, I have given you every herb bearing seed, which is upon the face of all the earth, and every tree, in the which is the fruit of a tree yielding seed; to you it shall be for meat. And to every beast of the earth, and to every fowl of the air, and to every thing that creepeth upon the earth, wherein there is life, I have given every green herb for meat: and it was so. Genesis 1:28-30

Although this authority was taken from Adam and Eve because of their sin, Jesus restored that authority back to us by defeating Satan on the cross. Today, we use that authority by faith.

As new covenant believers we have dominion over much more than just the earth. We have control over ourselves and any situation that pertains to us; and we have control over the demonic realm.

Ephesians 1 tells us that we have the same power that raised Christ Jesus from the dead, and because of that, all principalities and powers are under our feet! (See Eph. 1:19-22.) Jesus Himself is living inside of us. And with Jesus, comes *everything* else! We have everything we will ever need because He is everything we will ever need.

According as his divine power hath given unto us all things that pertain unto life and godliness, through the knowledge of him that hath called us to glory and virtue. 2 Peter 1:3

All things means exactly that: ALL things. We have healing, prosperity, love, joy, peace, mercy, forgiveness, faith, protection, deliverance, and His power within us. It's by faith that we manifest all of these things in our lives. But we need a revelation of this. If we don't know about something, how can it work for us?

That the communication of thy faith may become effectual by the acknowledging of every good thing which is in you in Christ Jesus. Philemon 6

Who we are and what we have cannot possibly work for us unless we *acknowledge* who we are and what we have. We must know it and believe it, then faith can work properly.

There are many whom some would call "control freaks." They love to be in control. They love to take charge. Some more aggressively than others, but we all have some of that in us. There's a desire to control meetings, personal conversations, decisions, and so forth. What we don't realize is that we actually have all the control we need because God has given it to us! We have control over every area of our lives. But this control is not to be used selfishly as in the examples just given.

Whenever we are in a conversation and we feel we must have the last word, that kind of control is completely selfish and void of God. It does not glorify God at all but only feeds our carnal flesh.

The control, or authority that God has given us, is to be used for one purpose only, and that is to glorify God on this earth; to bring attention to Him so that others will follow Him. We bring attention to Him by the victory people witness in our daily lives.

An example of this is the story I shared in chapter 5 about how I took authority over the hurricanes here in Florida. Through the power in me, which is Christ Himself, I have learned to take authority—His authority—and speak to the weather and get results. I had determined that our family did not have to be victims of another storm. If I could believe for safety through the hurricanes, then I could also believe that they would no longer hit Florida in the first place.

Whenever I'd see a television report of a hurricane coming toward Florida, I would lay my hands directly on the television and rebuke the hurricane, commanding it to go out into the sea. I refused to settle for another storm. I spoke to the storm, telling it that it did not have permission to come to Florida. Since that time—and it's been several years—there has never been a hurricane that touched the eastern coast of Florida. They tried but then headed another way, and it was because I used my God-given authority.

Because of this story, which I share in my book *God's Best Is for You Too!* there are many who see a storm on the horizon and actually call me to speak to it! Of course, they can do it themselves, but it's funny how people remember that I did this. When all the other homes around us had extensive damage and we had none, it brought the question to people's minds: *How could this happen?* And then I can tell them it's because of Jesus! I get to bring attention to Him.

I can share story after story of how we have taken our authority and it worked. My husband and I not only believe that we should tell people *what* they need to do, but also *how* to do it. People want practicality. This is how to take authority, and it comes straight from Scripture:

> *For verily I say unto you, That whosoever shall say unto this mountain, Be thou removed, and be thou cast into the sea; and shall not doubt in his heart, but shall believe that those things which he saith shall come to pass; he shall have whatsoever he saith. Therefore I say unto you, What things soever ye desire, when ye pray, believe that ye receive them, and ye shall have them. Mark 11:23-24*

The important word here is *say*. Saying is not thinking; it is speaking out loud. Bible teacher Kenneth Copeland said awhile back that the purpose of words is not for communication; it's for creative power. When God created the world, He spoke it into existence. This was how He used *His* authority, by speaking something into existence. We need to do the same.

This is what Jesus tried to convey to His disciples in this verse. He had spoken to the fig tree the day before, cursing it to die. The following day, it was withered and dead. The disciples were shocked, and this is when Jesus instructed them to speak to their mountains or problems in their lives. This was the whole point of the fig tree story. Jesus was getting ready to hand the baton to His disciples, and He was preparing them to take their authority when necessary.

This is interesting. Notice that verse 23 says ***but shall believe that those things which he says shall some to pass***, *he shall have whatsoever he saith (emphasis mine).* If we are speaking to something that may be hard for us to believe will actually happen, if we just believe in the power of our words, then that's a great start. If you have a hard time believing for the healing of cancer, for example, then start by believing in the power of your words as you cast the cancer out!

I have found that we need to take authority at the very onset of the problem. Sad to say, many Christians go into a whirlwind after bad news. They cry, complain, fall victim to fear and worry, and then after a day or two, they come to their senses and get into faith. It's always good that they finally get to a place of faith, but it would be better to never speak words of fear and worry in the first place, thus creating unbelief.

It's always better to live in a place where doubt and unbelief never even enter your mind. But most of the time, these thoughts do enter, and there is something we need to do when that happens.

I suffered from strep throat and sinus infections for years. I never knew I wasn't supposed to be sick; I never knew that Jesus died so I wouldn't have to suffer physical sickness. I was not taught what the Bible had to say about healing. Then I finally learned the truth. I knew I didn't have to suffer any longer! Soon came another bout of strep throat along with a sinus infection. I was miserable, but this time, I made a decision. I did not go to the doctor, although I was suffering tremendously. I learned about my authority and took my authority over the symptoms. After a couple of days the symptoms left, and I was well. It's been about ten years since then, and I have never had another strep throat. I refuse to allow it in my body.

Recently I had symptoms of another sinus infection. I know a lot more today than I did years ago, so I was spiritually fighting it, expecting it to leave. I became frustrated and mad because I felt that I failed and there was something I missed since I really do believe that I have been healed through Jesus.

So I asked the Lord why I got that sinus infection. I believe that I'm healed and absolutely know that sickness has no right to enter my body. In fact, I specifically remembered one day while I was vacuuming, I felt a very minor tickle in my throat and I immediately thought to myself how I never get colds anymore. I thought how I never get the flu or sinus infections or strep throat anymore. And I was happy about it. I was sort of snickering at the devil because I overcame these things.

The Lord showed me something about this whole situation. He reminded me of when I first got that tiny one-second tickle in my throat. What did I do? I thought to myself, *Hah, I never get sinus infections anymore.* But He said the problem was that I just thought about it! And I thought that was enough, but it wasn't. I needed to take my authority over that little symptom right there and then so that it couldn't come on me. It's not enough just to *think* that you are healed; you have to *speak* that you are healed! Tell that sickness "No!"

The Lord showed me clearly that sickness wanted to come on me, and it began very slowly. It's at that time that I should have put an end to it, but I didn't, and as a result I suffered terrible sinus symptoms for two days. It would have lasted a lot longer if I had not taken authority over it when I did, but I learned I never had to get it in the first place. I've learned to attack sickness on the onset.

As Christians, we have a God-given responsibility to use the authority given to us. We need to be bold and confident when standing against the enemy as we protect what is rightfully ours, guarding what Jesus died to give us. That is abundant life!

Chapter Fourteen

The Love Connection

A new commandment I give unto you, That ye love one another; as I have loved you, that ye also love one another.

John 13:34

Jesus calls us to love one another. He also tells us *how* to love one another. According to the above scripture, we are to love *as* He loves us. But in order for us to do this, we need to personally experience God's love toward us.

This chapter will cover three simple points: We must know that God loves us; we must know how to love others; and we must realize the importance and results of loving others.

It is a fact that God loves us, yet there are many in the body of Christ with a warped perception of this love. They will say that He loves them, but then they will also say that

He causes accidents, sickness, and diseases to happen to them because of that love.

Unfortunately, many Christians believe that God brings hardship on His children to teach them something; and they call that His "love." Some say that God is the author of trials in order to strengthen us. I don't know about you, but trials do not strengthen me; if anything, they weary me. What does strengthen me during a trial is relying on the awesome promises of God. It makes no sense at all that God would bring hardship on us. Think about how we treat our own children. Do we bring terrible trials on them to teach them patience? Do we make them cross a busy highway and get hit by a truck just to teach them to look both ways before they cross? No, because we love our children! The book of Romans alone uses the phrase *much more* at least seven times. If we love our children enough not to bring any harm to them, how *much more* will your heavenly Father love His children by not bringing harm to them?

If you were to ask people if they believed that God loved them, most, if not all, would say yes. But there is a difference between understanding it in your head and experiencing it in your heart.

And we have known and believed the love that God hath to us. God is love; and he that dwelleth in love dwelleth in God, and God in him. 1 John 4:16

The word *known* is translated "experience." If we haven't experienced God's love for us personally, then we just have head knowledge of Him. This means we can't love others because we can't give away what we don't have.

Much of the body of Christ believes that God's love fluctuates based on their performance. When they do right by God, He loves them more; when they mess up, He loves them less.

I remember a time when my relationship with God was not steady. Sometimes I felt strongly connected to the Lord in every way, and other times my relationship with Him felt dry, and I wasn't as enthusiastic about it. I asked the Lord about this, and He said that there was something deep in my subconscious that made me think I had displeased Him or made Him angry. I was running away from God just as Adam and Eve did when they sinned. I knew inside of me that this was the problem. The Lord asked me what it was that I thought may have displeased Him, but I didn't know.

We know the devil is succeeding when we feel guilty and condemned about something that we can't even remember!

God's love for us is constant. His love is based on who He is and not on what we do. As far as my children are concerned, it doesn't matter what they do or don't do; my love for them is constant.

Romans 8:38-39 tell us that nothing, not even our failings, can separate us from the love of God. This is what the grace of God is all about. He is never mad at us!

How much more does God have to do to show us that He loves us? He sent His sinless Son to suffer our punishment for sin and to free us from all self-righteousness, giving us His righteousness in return. We no longer have to perform for Him to get Him to love and accept us because He is not holding anything against us. He treats us as if we never sinned!

Bible teacher Arthur Meintjes shared his story of talking with the Lord one day and repeating the phrase, "I love You, Lord," several times. He was filled with such joy as he did this. But then he heard a voice say, "Arthur, I don't care if you love Me." Arthur began rebuking the enemy, but it was God speaking to him. The Lord told him He didn't care if Arthur loved Him. What He did care about was that Arthur knew just how much He loved him!

It's so important to God for us to know that He loves us. He gets much joy and pleasure when we love Him, but even if we never loved Him a day in our lives, it would never change the truth that He loves us.

> *Herein is love, not that we loved God, but that He loved us. 1 John 4:10*

We must know how to love others. Having a revelation of God's love for us will change the way we treat others; it's a progression. Again, we can't give away what we don't have. If the way we treat or respond to others is not improving, then we really are not grasping God's love for us.

> *Beloved, if God so loved us, we ought to love one another. 1 John 4:11*

Ephesians 5:1-2 tell us to *Be ye therefore followers of God, as dear children; and walk in love, as Christ also hath loved us.*

The word *follower* means "to imitate."

How can we know when we are not walking in love? I discussed these verses earlier in chapter 3, but let's take a quick look at Ephesians 4 once again:

> *Putting away lying, speak every man truth with his neighbor. (v. 25)*

When we lie we are not showing love to others, and this includes white lies. I have so many people tell me that it's okay to tell a white lie because it's a little lie, and it won't hurt anyone. But the Bible makes no distinction between types of lies; lying is lying, big or small.

> *Let him that stole steal no more. (v. 28)*

Stealing from others is another way to now show love. People feel violated and afraid when they are stolen from. How is this showing love?

> *Let no corrupt communication proceed out of your mouth…let all bitterness, and wrath, and anger, and clamour, and evil speaking, be put away from you, with all malice. (vv. 29, 31)*

If we operate in any of the ways listed in verses 29 and 31, we are not showing love toward others.

Ephesians 5:3 and on continue with actions that are the opposite of love, such as fornication, uncleanness, and covetousness.

Have you ever desired what other people have? Rather than being jealous, the proper attitude should be that we are happy for them. We should rejoice with them. It would be wise on our part to find out what they did to get where they are. And we must know that what God did for them He will also do for us. Jealousy and covetousness are not ways to love people.

An excellent scripture that confirms this is Romans 13:10:

Love worketh no ill to his neighbour: therefore love is the fulfilling of the law.

Bottom line is, would Jesus exhibit any of this behavior? No, of course not, and we need to imitate Him. But it shouldn't be hard for us to do. Remember, once we personally experience God's love, loving others becomes easier and easier.

My husband gave me beautiful diamond earrings one year for Valentine's Day. A few weeks later I was in a department store having fun trying on various costume jewelry earrings. A few days later I realized I had left one of my diamond earrings at the store and mistakenly took home one of the costume jewelry earrings I had tried on. Needless to say, I was a bit anxious to return to the store to see if my earring was still there.

The store had just completed a two-day major jewelry sale, so I just imagined what could have happened to my diamond earring. I prayed and believed that God would protect that earring, and He did. The following day I went to the store and noticed it immediately. At that moment I felt such an overwhelming sense of God's love. I was basking in it.

I shopped for a while and had a few items in my hand that I decided not to purchase, but one of the items belonged at the other end of the store. Most people would just place the item on the nearest rack rather than taking it back to where it belonged. But I was more than happy to take the time to do the right thing and return it to where I found it. I had just experienced God's love for me in such a way that I was pleased to do the right thing; it was easy.

Not putting the clothing back would not be showing love for others—in this case the employees. They would have to take the time to do it if I left the item just anywhere. I chose to love others as God loved me.

> *Herein is our love made perfect, that we may have boldness in the day of judgment: because as he is, so are we in this world. 1 John 4:17*

This is speaking of love. In our new born-again Spirit man, we are exactly like Jesus, including His love in us. It's there, so let's live in it! We really are just like Him in this life!

We must realize the importance and results of loving others. The first reason that loving others is important is because it's a witness to those around us.

> *A new commandment I give unto you, That ye love one another; as I have loved you, that ye also love one another. By this shall all men know that ye are my disciples, if ye have love one to another. John 13:34-35*

This does not say that people will know we are His disciples because of the clothes we wear, or because of how much we read our Bibles, or because of how many years we taught Sunday school. Loving others is the proof that we belong to Jesus.

Years ago my husband and I went to Madison Square Garden to see Bible teacher Creflo Dollar. We were there three hours early to make sure we got a decent seat up front. Many seats were reserved, especially in the center, for pastors and their families, so the best seat I could get was the twentieth row on the side. We left our Bibles on our chairs and went to purchase some books. The praise and worship began so we headed back to our seats only to find that our seats were taken by two ladies, and our Bibles had been tossed onto the floor.

These women had their hands raised in the air worshipping Jesus. I very nicely explained to one of the ladies that we were holding those seats when she began to lash out at me. She was on the verge of screaming at me, making sure I knew that I was not going to get my seats back. She made it a point to let me know that someone stole her seats up front so she was taking mine. All the while as she was yelling, her hand remained in the air praising God!

I was shocked, to say the least, but for a brief moment I saw the face of Jesus. I wanted so much to please Him with my reaction. I simply asked her for the Bibles and thanked her. I maintained my peace, and as I turned around all I could see that was still available was the "nose bleed" section of the arena, which, at that point was not a problem; I was just glad I was there.

As we were heading up to the seats a woman came up to me and very abruptly asked me what happened. I explained it to her, still keeping my peace. She told me to follow her. She was an usher and witnessed the entire episode. She took us to the third row, center section for our seats with all the pastors and their families. God is so good!

As I sat there I realized that with just one turn of my head, I could see that lady perfectly. I was tempted to turn and smile, but I didn't. Why? Because it wasn't necessary. I enjoyed the rest of the evening just relishing God's love for me once again. Because of my reaction, I was a witness to that usher. She knew I was a disciple of Jesus because I showed love to that woman. I would like to think I was a witness to those two ladies also.

The second reason why it's important to love others is because it brings us confidence.

Dear children, let's not merely say that we love each other; let us show the truth by our actions. Our actions will show that we belong to the truth, so we will be confident when we stand before God. 1 John 3:18-19 (New Living Translation)

Herein is love made perfect, that we may have boldness on the day of judgment: because as he is, so are we in this world. 1 John 4:17

Not only will we show others that we belong to Jesus, but it will give us great confidence when we stand before God someday. On the Day of Judgment, we can stand before Jesus with boldness and confidence and without shame. Because of Jesus we are free and clear of all judgment because of His love for us. Since we know and believe this we can love others freely and easily as He loves us. As He is so are we in this world.

Chapter Fifteen

The Power of Words

Death and life are in the power of the tongue: and they that love it shall eat the fruit thereof.

Proverbs 18:21

Words have power. I have taught many times on the power of our thoughts and how to think healthy, right thoughts according to the Word of God. It is important because our words are a result of our thoughts. As I mentioned earlier, a well-known Bible teacher once said that the primary purpose for words is not communication. Communication is important; after all, how will we know what's on each other's minds if we don't speak our thoughts out to one another? So, communication is necessary, but according to Scripture, it is not the primary purpose for our words.

The primary purpose is for the release of creative power. When God created the world He did it through words.

Our words can create good to happen, or they can create bad to happen. They literally create death or life. This is why it's important that we have the right kind of "speech life."

There are many Christians who are sick, poor, fearful, anxious, worried, and full of stress, and I think 90 percent of their problem is their speech life. I listen to people, and most bring on exactly what they think, which is eventually what they say. We must learn to use our words effectively. This is a challenge for me as well. The words we speak will either put us over or keep us in bondage, but it is our choice what we speak.

Today, many Christians have been taken captive by their own words; even by their own prayers. We've all done it at one time or another. We speak our problem rather than the answer, which in turn amplifies the problem and creates more unbelief. If you say "I'm sick," then you'll be sick; if you say "I'm afraid," then you'll be afraid; if you say "I'm worried," then you'll remain worried.

> *Death and life are in the power of the tongue: and they that love it shall eat the fruit thereof. Proverbs 18:21*

The original Greek word for *power* is *yad*. One of the meanings is "direction," so we can say that death or life will occur in our lives depending on the direction our tongue decides to take. This is totally up to us; it's our decision what we choose to say.

> *Even so the tongue is a little member, and boasteth great things. Behold, how great a matter a little fire kindleth. James 3:5*

You cannot start a fire with a full-size log. You have to start it with a thin piece of dried-out wood, then it begins to ignite. This is called kindling. Once the fire begins to kindle then you throw the log onto it.

We start with seemingly innocent words, such as, "I'm tired." This is your dried-out piece of wood. Then you repeat it over and over and the kindling begins. Then the devil throws the log on the fire. Why can he do this? Because we have given him permission by the words we speak. If not dealt with immediately, it's possible that the fire could get out of control like a wildfire.

This is what happens with our words. They can become a huge wildfire, which will bring tiredness and weariness day and night. Then people ask, "What's wrong with me? I think I should go see a doctor." There's nothing wrong with you that you haven't created with your own words. There is creative power in every word we speak.

There is a story in the first chapter of Luke that not only demonstrates the importance of our speech life but also of the great unmerited mercy and grace of God. It is the story of a certain priest named Zacharias and his wife, Elizabeth. They both were righteous before God and walked blameless in the commandments of the Lord (see v. 6). Elizabeth was barren, and they both resigned themselves to the fact that they would never have children because of their old age.

Holding the office of a priest, Zacharias went into the temple of the Lord to burn incense. It was there that he had a visitor. An angel of the Lord appeared to him with quite a message. Verses 13 through 17 reveal this great promise. The angel told him that their prayer was heard, and they would have a son. His name would be John. They would be joyful and glad and many would rejoice at his birth. The angel went on to say that their child would be great in the Lord's sight and would be filled with the Holy Spirit from his mother's womb. He would prepare the hearts of the people to receive the Lord. John the Baptist would be born to prepare the way of the Lord!

What a promise! I could imagine that Zacharias was scared when the angel appeared. To hear a message like this was probably quite shocking to him. Verse 18 says: *And Zacharias said unto the angel, Whereby shall I know this? for I am an old man, and my wife well stricken in years. The Message Bible* translates this as: *Do you expect me to believe this? I am an old man and my wife is an old woman!*

Zacharias and Elizabeth had been praying for a child for years, but when the Lord finally answered their prayer, Zacharias didn't believe it. This is a classic example of living by what we see rather than by what the Word of God says. The word of the Lord said they would have a child with awesome promises, but because of Zacharias' "natural" thinking, he just could not believe that word. Zacharias proved he didn't believe it by speaking out his unbelief. Because of his unbelief, God struck him dumb.

The lesson for us is that when a thought comes into our mind, we need to examine that thought before we speak it.

If the thought lines up with the Word of God, then speak it; if it doesn't, then be quiet (see James 1:19).

To be clear, however, God does *not* deal with us in this manner today. Because of the cross, we are now under a new covenant of grace and mercy rather than judgment. The book of Luke was still in the Old Testament dispensation, so people lived under the Law. God used the Law and brought punishment when it was broken, but only to show the people that they could never keep the whole Law. They needed a Savior who was still to come.

God's reaction to Zacharias was conducive to everyone living under the Law. God dealt with people differently because of that. But the principle of how God feels about our words still remains.

Luke 1:20 is clear as to why Zacharias' mouth was shut, but I believe there was also another reason the Lord did this. Zacharias already had problems believing the word of the Lord. How do you think he would have handled the next nine months of his wife's pregnancy? Because he started out in unbelief, Zacharias would have continued to speak doubt and unbelief over the entire situation.

Can't you just hear him: "How can we do this? We are too old. Why couldn't God answer our prayer years ago when we were younger? How will Elizabeth handle this? She will have to be bedridden for nine months. This will be too much for her. We are too old to get up for 2 a.m. feedings. We can't afford to hire help. This will be hard, very hard." These are all words of unbelief.

I believe it was God shielding him from messing up His whole plan. Not only was Zacharias in unbelief, but God didn't want him speaking his unbelief onto others, including Elizabeth. God's mercy protected His own plan. This should reveal to us what God thinks about what we say. The Lord went to great lengths to keep Zacharias from speaking unbelief, which could have ruined His plan for the entire world!

It was of extreme importance that John the Baptist be born. Malachi 4:6 says that if John did not fulfill his mission, then the earth would be cursed forever:

> *And he shall turn the heart of the fathers to the children, and the heart of the children to their fathers, lest I come and smite the earth with a curse.*

There would be no salvation for the world! We could say that if Zacharias continued speaking unbelief, John may have never been born! Thank God that He continually urges, encourages, and exhorts us to speak faith rather than unbelief because He knows that whatever we say will either employ His angels (see Ps. 103:20) or demonic powers to bring destruction to the very situation we want to get rid of!

God will not override what we say. He chose to give us a free will to make our own decisions as to what we do and say. If we choose to speak unbelief, He will not judge us for it because Jesus took the wrath of God onto Himself at the cross (see 1 John 2:2), but we will reap the consequences of what we say. Our words will come to pass. Any words we speak, whether death or life, will affect our lives.

I love what happens to Zacharias once John is born. He decides to obey God and name his son John as the angel declared to him nine months before.

At that moment Zacharias' mouth was opened, and he spoke and praised God (see Luke 1:64). Filled with the Holy Ghost, Zacharias spoke to the people, telling of all the wonderful things John would accomplish as he prepared the people for the coming of the Lord (see vv. 68-79). What a difference nine months can make!

> *Even God, who quickeneth the dead and calleth those things that which be not as though they were. Romans 4:17*

God calls things that aren't as though they already happened. Shouldn't we be doing the same? When we become born again, we receive every bit of God inside of us, including the faith of God!

> *I am crucified with Christ: nevertheless I live; yet not I, but Christ liveth in me: and the life which I now live in the flesh, I live by* **THE FAITH** *of the Son of God, who loved me, and gave himself for me. Galatians 2:20 (emphasis mine)*

If we have been given the faith of God, then we should be able to speak those things that aren't as those they were! Most Christians, however, speak what they have rather than what they want. An example would be if your child was failing in a class. Instead of speaking that he is failing, although that may be the fact, speak the truth, which is that he is an "A" student. This is speaking those things that aren't as though they were. In time, that child will be an "A" student. We did this exact same thing with our son years ago; he became an "A" student, and his words to us were: "That's amazing because I never did anything different to get that 'A.'" But we did; we spoke that our son was an "A" student. We wouldn't settle for anything less.

Years ago a family situation occurred that led me to witness something being done to someone else that I did not like. It was wrong, and even God would agree that it was wrong. Heading home on a three-day drive from vacation gave me much time to think about it and to continue to think about it and even occasionally share it with Al. Rather than bringing those thoughts captive to Jesus and taking authority over them, I allowed them to magnify in my mind.

I had imagined that when I finally arrived home all I wanted to do was go into a private area and let it all out to God. I was hurting and sad and upset. I wanted to tell the Lord all that had happened, tell Him how I felt, and just ask Him to make me feel better.

I was looking forward to this time with God. By the time we got home, my thoughts had become so toxic they were coming out of my mouth. I desperately needed to get with God. I finally made it to my prayer room. I began walking around in my room, saying, "This is it, Lord, I'm about to tell You everything." (As if He didn't already know.) I had waited a long time for this moment.

I was about to let it all out when I realized the Lord would not allow me to say anything about it! I couldn't get the first word out of my mouth. He told me, "You know what to do, and you know what to say." I knew exactly what He was talking about, but I was trying to ignore it. I wanted to pretend that I had a right to have a pity party with Him so He could pat me on the back and tell me I'm doing a great job and cry with me.

He told me what to do: "Speak My Word because that's what I understand." How upset I was at that moment because I wanted so badly to speak words of negativity, words of death, and of all the hurts and fears and worry. But if I did that it would only have magnified the entire problem. I should have put the fire out while driving home when it was only kindling!

I was biting my lip trying to hold back from saying what my flesh wanted to say. But I knew better. On purpose, I chose to speak the Word of God, declaring that He was in control of the situation and that He loved these people who had done wrong. I declared that He was working on them and bringing revelation to their lives. I spoke that the situation would change and the angels were on the job. Anything the Bible said about it, I spoke it and did it all with thanksgiving.

I was saying it with tears streaming down my face because it was a battle. I had a choice. I'm so glad that God was right there to help me and to pick me up and teach me. When I left that room, I felt God give me a pat on the back anyway. He hugged me; He was pleased!

But what did my response accomplish? It didn't make God love me any more, but it got the devil out of the picture. He no longer was involved in this situation. Things are so much better that I don't even pray about what had happened anymore. God is so faithful. He is our cheerleader, always cheering us on to do the right thing.

We need to start speaking solutions rather than problems. Let's bring life into our situations. We will have what we say.

Chapter Sixteen

The Thorn

And lest I should be exalted above measure through the abundance of the revelations, there was given to me a thorn in the flesh, the messenger of Satan to buffet me, lest I should be exalted above measure. For this thing I besought the Lord thrice, that it might depart from me. And he said unto me, My grace is sufficient for thee: for my strength is made perfect in weakness.

2 Corinthians 12:7-9

I believe that this scripture is one of the most misunderstood scriptures in the Bible. The prevalent thinking is that Paul had a physical ailment of some kind. Some say he had eye trouble; others say he was sick. It really doesn't matter what kind of sickness; it's just believed he had a physical limitation.

People always refer to this scripture when they are suffering from some kind of illness. They have prayed to God to heal them, but they remain sick. They believe that sometimes God says yes to healing, and other times He says no. Many who are suffering physically and are not getting healed will refer to Paul's thorn in the flesh and say, "After all, God said no to Paul, and he asked Him three times." This kind of thinking is just not scriptural.

God will not say no to what He already said yes to! First Peter 2:24 states: *by whose stripes ye were healed.* God says yes to healing, so this passage could not be talking about God saying no to healing. He has already healed everyone! He wants everyone well and whole. Even if Paul's thorn was sickness, it doesn't line up with what God says about healing. But it certainly is not talking about any kind of physical sickness.

Many in the body of Christ believe that God brings sickness and disease to His children either to teach them something, or to punish them, or to strengthen them. None of this is true. Those who believe this, though, will also go to great lengths to try to get better, like going to the doctor or taking medicine.

There is nothing wrong with going to a doctor, but if they think that the sickness was from God, or that God wants them to stay sick, why are they going against the will of God by trying to get better? It makes no sense. The apostle Paul said it was a messenger of Satan that came to buffet him; not a messenger of God. God doesn't bring sickness, and He does not say no to healing.

I misunderstood this scripture myself at one time, but my eyes were opened years ago when I learned to be careful not to take any scripture out of its context. It's obvious in chapters 10, 11, and 12 that Paul was dealing with critics. He had a lot of opposition and began defending himself. He defended himself only because this is what his critics understood. He had to get down on their level in order to communicate because it was the only way he could reach them. This was not boasting on Paul's part. He was pushed to the limit by his opponents. He spoke foolishly like a lost person (see 2 Cor. 11:21).

> *Have I committed an offence in abasing myself that ye might be exalted, because I have preached to you the gospel of God freely? 2 Corinthians 11:7*

In other words, Paul couldn't understand why people would come out against him while he was preaching the Gospel to them without taking any money. In fact, that's *why* he didn't take money from them—to stop his critics. There were many false prophets who *were* taking their money. Paul was selfless, and they still criticized him. He was being severely persecuted.

In verses 23-27 Paul continues to tell the Corinthians of all he had suffered for them and how he was imprisoned, beaten, weary, hungry, thirsty, cold and naked, stoned, shipwrecked, and in danger of robbers, Jews, and unbelievers. Paul was boasting of his *sufferings* for the cause of Christ and not because of his accomplishments, as the false prophets were doing. He knew it was all Jesus working through him and that God was to get the glory because of that.

> *But he that glorieth, let him glory in the Lord. 2 Corinthians 10:17*

It's obvious up to this point that Paul suffered a tremendous amount of persecution. Why was he being persecuted? Because he was preaching the true Gospel.

Yea, and all that will live godly in Christ Jesus shall suffer persecution. 2 Timothy 3:12

I remember a T-shirt I used to have showing a school of fish all going in the same direction, but there was one fish heading in the opposite direction. The caption on the shirt read: "Go against the flow." If we choose to live godly in this world, we can be sure to receive persecution. It's a guarantee. We are like that one fish going against the majority. And if we are not being persecuted in some way, we need to take a serious look at our Christianity.

Paul's thorn in the flesh was not sickness; in fact, if it was sickness, then God would have healed him. It was persecution, and we aren't redeemed from persecution. Three times in the Old Testament the term "thorn in the flesh" was used, and three times it referred to people as persecutors. In Numbers 33:55, Joshua 23:13, and Judges 2:3, God warned His people that if they left any of the inhabitants alive they would become "thorns" in their sides.

Paul's thorn in the flesh was from Satan. The demons stirred up the people against Paul. Why? Because Paul was being exalted *by the people*. Paul wasn't exalting Paul;

the people were exalting Paul. Many were amazed at his teachings and were getting saved. He was becoming very popular, and the devil took notice. It was never Paul's intention to exalt himself.

> *For though I would desire to glory, I shall not be a fool; for I will say the truth: but now I forbear, lest any man should think of me above that which he seeth me to be, or that heareth of me. 2 Corinthians 10:6*

Paul was saying that he would love to share the revelations he received from the Lord, but he wouldn't do it because he didn't want man to exalt him in any way. He wanted only God to be exalted. Paul was not puffed up about these revelations; in fact, verse 5 says: *Of such a one will I glory: yet of myself I will not glory, but in mine infirmities.*

While studying this, I was shocked as I read several other Bible versions, such as *The Amplified*, the *New International Version*, the *New American Standard Version*, the *New Living Translation*, and *The Message Bible*. All these versions clearly state that Paul was given this thorn to "keep him from becoming conceited" or to "keep him from becoming proud." *The Message Bible* reads: *So I wouldn't get a big head I was given the gift of a handicap to keep me in constant touch with my limitations (v. 7).* Since when is a handicap a gift? Read these versions for yourself.

I now can understand why this wrong doctrine is being taught in our churches. Those who preach on this scripture do so from these various translations. I understand why they are saying what they are saying, but if kept in its context, it means something entirely different. I am not promoting a certain translation, but many of them are incorrect. *The King James Version* is accurate in this passage. But still, the verse must be kept in its context!

Some think that it was a sickness because of the word *infirmities*, but Paul used that word in association with his hardships. In chapter 11, after he describes all his hardships, of which there was no sickness, he calls them infirmities.

Ask yourself this question: Why would God call Paul on the road to Damascus, have him filled with the Holy Spirit, tell him that he was called to preach the Gospel to the Gentiles (Acts 9:15), and then keep him sick so he couldn't do it? Really? How do we see God? The devil was trying to steal Paul's assignment. He doesn't want any of us to fulfill the call on our life. John 10:10 says the devil steals, but God gives abundant life!

> *The thief cometh not, but for to steal, and to kill, and to destroy: I am come that they might have life, and that they might have it more abundantly.*

Abundant life is a life full of purpose and meaning, and that's what the devil wanted to steal from Paul. So now that we understand Paul's thorn was not sickness, let's look at 2 Corinthians 12:8-9:

> *For this thing I besought the Lord thrice, that it might depart from me. And he said unto me: My grace is sufficient for thee: for my strength is made perfect in weakness.*

Paul was asking God to stop his persecutors! Paraphrased, God said this to him: "Paul, you aren't redeemed from persecution, but you have My grace to deal with it!" Simple. Persecution will come, but we are to find our strength in Him.

Paul says something interesting in verse 10: *Therefore I take pleasure in infirmities, in reproaches, in necessities, in persecutions, in distresses for Christ's sake: for when I am weak, then am I strong.*

Paul is saying that when he is weak, then he is strong. How could he be weak and strong at the same time? Paul's flesh was weak, but his Spirit man, where Christ and all His fullness dwells, resides inside of him. All the strength that would ever be needed is right there. God was telling Paul that when he was weak, then God would show Himself strong. He was telling him to use His grace (strength) to persevere.

The bottom line is that God wants you well, not sick. Sadly, most Christians choose to believe that Paul's thorn was sickness and that God refused to heal him so they can rationalize why they are not getting well. But the truth is that we have been given power and authority over all sickness and disease, but many are too passive to be bothered using it. So this becomes a convenient theology for them, yet unscriptural. What ***IS*** biblical is that *all things are under our feet (Eph. 1:22)*! Amen!

Chapter Seventeen

Umbrellas of Love

For the gifts and calling of God are without repentance.

Romans 11:29

What is God's will for me? I know He has a plan for me, but I have no idea what it could be. What is His purpose for my life? If you are a serious Christian, then I know you've asked yourself these questions.

I've come across many Christians over the years who love the Lord and want to serve Him. They are excited about their faith and want to tell the whole world how good God is. I think that's great! This happens especially with new born-again believers. Once they've had a taste of the love and goodness of God, they can't wait to serve Him.

Although this is admirable, we need to be cautious. God does have a plan for everyone, but with that plan comes timing. I've seen ministries over the years grow and flourish, and I've seen others grow then crumble to nothing. I've seen smaller ministries that never seemed to grow and then eventually closed their doors. I've also seen individual Christians suffer one disappointment after another as they try to *do* something for the Lord but fail in their endeavors.

I believe the main reason for this is that we tend to get ahead of God. We can't speed up God's plan for us; it's going to happen when He decides. He has a time for everything. The problem arises when we don't wait. We go out after something rather than just wait for God to bring it to us. The Lord may put passions and desires in our hearts for years before they ever come to fruition.

The following true story illustrates the beauty of waiting on God, hearing His voice, and obeying a simple command.

Helping others was a part of Robin's heart. It seemed as though God had given her a desire for missions work. Or maybe she just had a passion for children, or she may have had a burden for the poor.

Whatever it was that was leading her, Robin took this God-given desire and chose to attend Bible college to learn all she could and to develop a precious relationship with Jesus Christ, who would one day lead her to fulfill the plan and purpose He had ordained for her.

> *And be not conformed to this world: but be ye transformed by the renewing of your mind, that ye may prove what is that good, and acceptable, and perfect, will of God. Romans 12:2*

Remember the story of Mary and Martha? Jesus visited them in their home, and Martha was busy preparing the meal while Mary sat at the feet of Jesus, soaking in His words. Martha became upset because she was doing all the physical work, so she told Jesus to get Mary to help her. But instead, Jesus replied, *Martha, Martha, thou art careful and troubled about many things: But one thing is needful: and Mary hath chosen that good part, which shall not be taken away from he (Luke 10:41-42).*

Like Mary, Robin chose the good part—the better part, sitting under the Word of God for two years. In her second year of school she went on a missions trip to Nicaragua with a ministry called Ambassadors to the Nations. Prior to her trip she was gathering last-minute essentials at a local store. The Lord spoke three simple words to her: "Buy an umbrella."

What was unusual about this was that Robin never owned an umbrella because she always loved to get wet in the rain! She didn't quite understand the instruction because Nicaragua's weather was over 100 degrees with no chance of any rain. But she obeyed and purchased a $5 umbrella.

On her first day in Nicaragua she did not pack her umbrella in her backpack. She also did not pack it on the second day. But on the third day God told her to pack her umbrella. So she did, even though there wasn't a cloud in the sky.

She was standing on the shoreline where there was a boat dedication in progress. The Lord told her to look out onto the water. She immediately saw a boat with two women on it. One of the ladies was using an umbrella to shield herself from the intense sun. The other woman didn't have an umbrella. The Lord spoke to her again, saying, "Go give your umbrella to that woman." It was for the sun, not the rain! She immediately obeyed, walked across the rocks, got the ladies' attention, and gave them her umbrella. They were full of joy!

Robin could have disregarded what she heard from the Lord because she knew it wasn't going to rain. It's so important that our reasoning doesn't get in the way of what God tells us to do. She could have reasoned herself right out of God's will. There may be times when God will tell us to do something that makes no sense at all. We need to just do it and not worry about it. In fact, it's none of our business what God does with it; just do it.

Robin herself was full of joy when she gave the umbrella away, so she began praying about it. The Lord said: "Keep doing it." When she got back to America, she began purchasing $5 umbrellas.

Some time went by, and the Lord spoke to her again, saying, "Go to the camp meeting." Robin had no idea what that meant; she had never heard of a camp meeting before. But just a couple of days later she received a magazine that advertised a camp meeting in Charlotte, North Carolina.

Andrew Wommack, the founder of the Bible college she attended, had been preaching at this same camp meeting for over twenty-five years. She also discovered that the church hosting the meeting served as the headquarters for Ambassadors to the Nations, the ministry through which she had taken her missions trip to Nicaragua!

She was excited! During this entire time she was spreading the word about her amazing experience in Nicaragua. To her surprise, she began receiving umbrellas from all over the country. There were many who sent her donations so she could purchase the umbrellas. People also donated T-shirts and Bibles.

She wanted to bring all the donations to the camp meeting to help fill Ambassadors to the Nations' containers that were being sent to Nicaragua. But she didn't have a car to drive there, so she began praying for one. One thing we can be sure of is if God tells us to do something, He will provide everything we need to accomplish it.

In just a short time, God provided her with a car, so she headed to Charlotte with over 100 umbrellas and numerous Bibles and T-shirts! She moved to Charlotte,

North Carolina, and interned for Ambassadors to the Nations.

There are many Christians who can't wait to get out of Bible college so they could start their own ministry. They have zeal, but many don't understand that they need to wait on God for direction. Robin did. She was not aggressively working to get a ministry started; she was just living her Christian life, and God brought it to her.

Years ago a Christian friend told me: "If I only knew what God's will was for me, then I would do it." That's great, but let's not forget that God is *looking* to reveal His plan to us. My husband had a plumbing business, and he was very eager to inform his workers about the plans he had for the houses he was working on. He wanted them to know all the details. God is the same way. He wants to get the information to us; He wants to get His plan to us. After all, how can we possibly fulfill that plan if we don't know what it is? He may not tell us everything at once simply because we couldn't handle it all. But He will direct us step by step along the way.

Robin stayed sensitive to God's still small voice, and although she didn't understand the "why" at the time, she simply obeyed. God brought this ministry to her. Her mind isn't on the future as much as it is on the here-and-now and what God is telling her to do day by day.

What should we do in the meantime while we wait for God's direction? Let's do what Jesus did:

> *How God anointed Jesus of Nazareth with the Holy Ghost and with power: who went about doing good, and healing all that were oppressed of the devil; for God was with him. Acts 10:38*

Jesus simply went about doing good. He didn't intentionally set up a ministry. He didn't advertise Himself. He just went about doing good. He healed all who were oppressed, and as He met the needs of others, His following grew larger and larger. But He never tried to make that happen. He just obeyed the Father daily, and it was His Father who brought the people to Him.

We need to let God do it. Robin did! She was going about doing good by taking a trip to Nicaragua to meet the needs of the people, and that's where her ministry began. It was all Jesus. Robin just heard and obeyed and now look how many people in Nicaragua are being blessed because of her!

This is only part of Robin's Story; she has experienced tremendous physical healing from the Lord and has gathered thousands of umbrellas through a series of unique ideas that the Lord has given her. It is Jesus' heart to bless others, and we, His children, are privileged to be chosen to bring those blessings to others.

Chapter Eighteen

What If?

And let the peace (soul harmony which comes) from Christ rule (act as umpire continually) in your hearts [deciding and settling with finality all questions that arise in your minds, in that peaceful state] to which as [members of Christ's] one body you were also called [to live]. And be thankful (appreciative), [giving praise to God always].

Colossians 3:15 (AMP)

Have you ever asked a question that began with "What if?" I have many times. Although we can be asking about something positive, such as, "What if I had a million dollars?" usually it's a wondering of the future in some negative way.

Here are some positive "What if's": "What if we lived in a ten million-dollar house with a huge pool, a waterfall, and a Jacuzzi? What if I became president? What if I owned the most expensive car in the world? What if I could buy anything I wanted at any time with no restrictions? What if I was the smartest person in the world? What if I never had any physical problems and never had to go to the doctor?" All positive, right?

Now here are some negative "What if's": "What if the economy collapses? What if I get the flu? What if I lose my job? What if I get sick? What if the baby I'm carrying is not healthy? What if I need to have surgery one day? What if I get into a car accident? What if the roller coaster that I'm riding breaks down while I'm on it? What if a nuclear bomb hits America? What if my family doesn't get saved?"

When we ask a "What if" question it is usually a negative thought, but what's really behind it is fear and worry concerning those things coming to pass. It's what I call 'an evil foreboding.' Foreboding means just that—a feeling of evil to come or an unfavorable omen.

The good news is when we begin thinking on negative things, there is a way out. According to God's Word, we can be free from fear in every way.

Of course, these "What if's" begin in our mind, in our thought life. Our thoughts are powerful. They can create positive or negatives in our life.

Here's an example of just how powerful they are. You get a call from your doctor's office telling you that your test results are in, and you should call them as soon as possible.

The first thing you think is *What if this is really bad news? Why do they want a call back right away?* You may begin thinking of several things it could be, imagining the worst. Or, you can get into denial and say: "This is just routine. I'll call when I get around to it." Or you can put your faith to work instead and say, "I am healed; I walk in divine health."

You choose one of the above. If you choose fear, you begin thinking *I'm sick*. Then you suddenly feel sick and even think you may die. Thoughts very quickly jump into your mind about the disease and how it will play out in your life and how it will affect others. You then think of how you would handle it day by day. And before you know it, you're planning your funeral!

So, you finally call your doctor, and he says all is fine. Suddenly, you feel great! Every ounce of fear and worry just left your body. You are at total peace and filled with joy. (Example paraphrased from *Switch on Your Brain,* Baker Books Publisher, Dr. Caroline Leaf.)

Something similar happened to me when I ran a children's ministry in my home many years ago. Each week forty to sixty children came to my house for snacks, Bible study, sports, and so forth. I remember one day all the children were outside with my volunteers, and I was cleaning up inside. One of the children ran into the house screaming, "Joey got hit by a car!"

That was it; I thought I would die at that moment. Every ounce of fear rose up in me. I felt faint; I felt like my heart was being squeezed. I became so paralyzed with fear that I couldn't go outside. I began gasping for air, my head was spinning, and every ounce of strength was taken from me. This is what fear can do to a person!

But strangely enough, no one else came in to get me. I waited and waited because I just couldn't bring myself to go outside and see this horrific thing that I was just told had happened.

Then one of my volunteers came in, and she seemed happy. I told her what one of the children just said, and she replied, "Oh, yeah, one of the other kids bumped into him in the Little Tykes car." Oh my goodness! It was a plastic car that hit the little boy!

Immediately, and I mean immediately, I came back to life. All fear instantly left me, and my strength and peace returned as fast as it had left. It was only my thoughts that brought that fear; it was not reality at all. I thought this was a great example of what our thoughts can do to us. Your brain actually becomes what you focus on, which produces how you feel physically and mentally.

Our imaginations can run wild; our minds will go anywhere we allow them to go. If we dwell on a negative possibility long enough, the thought then becomes toxic, which can create physical sickness in our lives. Author Dr. Caroline Leaf is a scientist and a born-again Christian. She writes in her book, *Switch on Your Brain,* that we are free to make choices about how we focus our attention, which in turn affects how the chemicals, proteins, and wiring of our brain change and function.

A person who is depressed is told he or she has a chemical imbalance. Years ago I did not believe a person could have a chemical imbalance, but that was because of my lack of knowledge on the subject. The chemical imbalance is created when our thoughts become toxic enough to create what Dr. Leaf calls "chemical chaos."

There are two ways to fix this chemical chaos: We can take medication to start stabilizing the chemicals in our brains, or we can do what the Bible teaches, which is to renew our minds to what the Word of God says about the situation (see Rom. 12:2).

It's okay to choose the medication route, as long as God has been invited into your situation. Then He can work with you to heal you. Dr. Leaf made the awesome point that we are wired for love and for the positive. This is the way God made us. It makes sense because God Himself is positive and is love (see 1 John 4:16). The Bible says we are made in His image.

> *So God created man in his own image, in the image of God created he him; male and female created he them. Genesis 1:27*

Other scientists also agree that we are wired for love. Dr. Leaf explains in her book, *The Gift in You*, when a negative thought that creates fear arises, 1400 chemical and physical responses occur in the brain that disrupt our thinking, producing stress. Why? Because our bodies were not made for fear. Fear is *not* a normal part of our bodies! The chemicals then go into disarray. This is what causes the chemical chaos, which can lead to all sorts of physical and emotional problems (*The Gift in You*, pp. 155-7).

In Matthew 6:25-34, we learn not to be worried about provision:

> *Take no thought for your life, what ye shall eat, or what ye shall drink; nor yet for your body, what ye shall put on. Is not the life more than meat, and the body than raiment? (v. 25)*

The word *thought* means "to be anxious; to be troubled with cares, to look out for a thing—like an evil foreboding." Here, God is telling us not to be anxious or fearful about the future! Jesus talked about the birds of the air and how they don't have to work for their food because God takes care of them; He then asked us, "How much more will your heavenly Father take care of you?" Worrying is not going to add any years to your life, and it certainly will not solve your problems.

He then asked, "Why worry about clothing?" He pointed out the lilies of the field and how they grow without working at it. He was saying that if He clothes the grass of the field and the lilies, shouldn't He much more clothe us?

This is a trust issue with God. If we worry about our future, then we are not trusting Him. We are not taking Him at his Word. Fear is the opposite of faith. Faith can't work where there is fear. Fear stems from unbelief in God's Word. If we don't believe God's Word, fear will come.

The following is a testimony of a man named Mike who works as a phone counselor at Andrew Wommack Ministries. One day Mike noticed a red scab on his left side under his shoulder. It was small, and he thought nothing of it. He tried to treat it with creams but that didn't help. Sometimes the scab would ooze with blood. His pastor told him he should go to the doctor, which he did. The doctors seemed concerned, but at this point Mike still thought nothing of it. Then he received a diagnosis that the scab was cancerous.

Can you imagine the "What if's" that went through Mike's mind? "What if this kills me?" was one possibility. When Mike received the news, he said that fear gripped his heart. He said it was as if a hand squeezed his heart really hard. He went to his pastor but just told him the diagnosis, not saying anything about the fear that struck him. His pastor said, "Mike, you can have it removed if you want, or you can believe God for healing, but before that, you need to get rid of the fear!"

Mike realized right then and there that he was now fighting two issues; not one. He knew that God was capable of healing him, so that wasn't even much of an issue to him compared to the dreaded fear! He also knew that this fear was exactly the thing that would keep him from receiving his healing, because fear stems from unbelief. So now he had the job of dealing with the fear. He knew once that was gone, he could then enjoy his healing.

So what did he do? He immersed himself in learning about God's love for him. He struggled with fear on and off for eight years as this tumor grew and grew. But then he got a revelation of how much God loved him, and from that point on, it took only eight months for the tumor to diminish day by day until it was completely gone. He is now totally healed!

But He did something about it. He invested his time into learning how much God really loved him and was on his side. His study developed confidence in this loving God; a God who, because of His love, would never let him down. (You can read more about Mike's testimony at www.awmi.net. Click on "Healing Testimonies.")

Continuing in Matthew 6:32, Jesus says that the Father already knows all the things we have need of. Jesus exhorts us to *seek ye first the kingdom of God, and his righteousness; and all these things shall be added unto you (v. 33).* What things was He speaking of? The things noted in the previous verses. Simply put, if we put God first in our lives, He will take care of all our needs.

This is what Mike did. He put God first and dedicated hours each day to learning about God's love for Him. Once you are convinced of His love for you, there really is nothing to fear. Mike conquered fear, and once he did, he began to see his healing taking place.

One day I was thinking on these terms and God said to me, "Don't ask yourself 'What if?' It's 'What ***is***' that's important."

Then He said to me, "It is well." What a positive God! His Word is positive. This brought to mind the song "It Is Well with My Soul" written by Horatio Spafford.

This hymn was written following a series of major tragedies in Spafford's life. His only son died from scarlet fever, and he lost his money because of the great Chicago fire and the collapse of the economy. He had planned to travel to Europe with his family on the *SS Ville du Havre*, but he was delayed so he sent his family ahead of him. While crossing the Atlantic, the ship sank after a collision, which led to the death of his four daughters. His wife survived and sent him the infamous telegram, "Saved alone." Shortly afterward, as Spafford traveled to meet his grieving wife, he wrote the following words, which became the first verse of the hymn, at the exact location where his daughters died.

When peace like a river, attendeth my way
When sorrows like sea billows roll
Whatever my lot, Thou hast taught me to say
It is well, it is well with my soul.

What would we do if the same happened to us? Would we write a song proclaiming that all that had happened was well with our soul? The only way we could would be through faith, realizing that no matter what happens, God still loves us and will never leave us. We must understand that the devil caused this tragedy; this did not come from God.

Second Kings chapter 4 tells the story of the Shunammite woman who cared for the prophet Elisha each time he came to her town. She gave him a room and sustained him. One day her son fell sick working in the field. He was brought to her, and he died in her lap.

She immediately pursued the prophet. She went to get a donkey and servant from her husband, telling him that she needed to go to the man of God. Her husband asked her why. She answered, *It shall be well (v. 23)*. She never told him the problem. I'm sure she felt fear, but she spoke only victory!

Elisha the prophet saw her coming and sent his servant to ask her if it was well with her, well with her husband, and well with her child. She replied, *It is well (v. 26)*. How could she do this? She had confidence in Almighty God.

She spoke God's words of faith rather than doubt, fear, and unbelief. The result of her faith was that the prophet raised the child from the dead.

We should never fear the future but rather understand that no matter what happens in life, God will never stop loving us. We need to make a decision to settle all questions that may arise in our minds and maintain our peace, which comes from the Lord. And always remain thankful, giving praise to our God. God is more than able to handle our future. Trust Him.

Chapter Nineteen

Why?

For I know the thoughts that I think toward you, saith the LORD. thoughts of peace, and not of evil, to give you an expected end.

Jeremiah 29:11

Many times we will ask the question "Why?" looking for a reason behind bad news. Some will respond, "There's a reason for everything." I agree with that, but we must make sure we answer the "Why?" question correctly, according to the Word of God. When people use this phrase, it's as if they believe that God had something to do with a particular evil event. Although it is not directly expressed this way, the underlying meaning is that God knows a lot more than we do, which is true. But they imply that, in His infinite wisdom, which we could never understand, He enforced an evil act for a really important reason—one that will only be revealed to us in heaven someday.

A good example of this kind of thinking happened recently when a high school boy was hit by a car and killed while riding his bike to work. Friends, relatives, pastors, and teachers all said that God took his life and had a reason for doing so. It was even said that this was the "contract" that God made for this boy before he was ever born. (God had a contract out on this boy?) So the reason he died is because God just decided it to be so.

Some believed this was God's plan for this young man's life—a plan for the life that God gave him, only to be cut short, and in such a painful way. People said it's just too mysterious to understand all the reasons why God would do this. But after all, He knows best. The truth is, those who saw this young man moments before he was hit noticed he was riding recklessly. He did not go to the corner and wait for a good opportunity to cross the street but steered into the middle of the highway as cars were coming both ways. He didn't use wisdom, which would have saved his life. It wasn't God who killed him.

I am sure many good things came out of this one incident. Some may have thought of the reality that life could end at any moment and made some changes to start appreciating things in their own lives, such as their families, their friends, or their jobs. Some could have realized that they needed a Savior to forgive them of their sins and became born again; others may have started teaching Sunday school to invest in the lives of young people.

Many good and positive things can come out of any bad situation, and this is one of the reasons that some think God had to be involved in some way, because so much good came out of it. But to credit God as the author of any tragedy is not what the Bible teaches.

> *For I know the thoughts that I think toward you, saith the LORD, thoughts of peace, and not of evil, to give you an expected end. Jeremiah 29:11*

It's important to look at the original Greek meanings of words in order to get the full impact of the truth that God wants to reveal to us.

In this verse, *thoughts* means "plan, purpose, or intervention." *Think* means "to plan, devise, impute, esteem, and value." *Peace* is translated "with family and with God, completeness, safety, health, prosperity, and contentment."

Evil is defined as "bad, malignant, unpleasant, pain, misery, unhappiness, displeasing, worse than, wicked, distress, injury, and calamity." And *expected* means "things hoped for; outcome."

Based on these definitions, we can then conclude that this verse is saying that God knows the plans and purposes that were originated by Him; that He thinks very highly of, and imputes toward us, plans of peace with God and each other, plans of safety, health, prosperity, contentment, and completeness, and not of evil, bad, malignant, unpleasant, pain, misery, unhappiness, displeasing, worse than, wicked, distress, injury, or calamity to give us hope in our final outcome.

This sounds to me like God is good; He is very good; He is only good! He is good all the time. His plans are good. To say that God ordains evil is a gross misrepresentation of the character of God.

A few years ago my husband shattered his pelvis. He fell off a four-foot ladder while fixing an air-conditioning vent. During his recovery I received a phone call from a Christian friend. She told me that God did this to Al to try to get him to slow down so he could get closer to God. I was shocked! She said God has ways we can never understand and that Al should take God's advice and slow down.

Unfortunately, this is the prevalent thinking in the body of Christ today. First of all, Al already was close to God. Second, I would think that if God was trying to get a message to Al, He could come up with a better way than to crush his pelvis; after all, He is God! So God put us under a huge trial, broke Al's bones, took our money, and stole our time—all because He wanted Al closer to Him because He loves him so much!

The reason why he fell was because he ignored the promptings of the Holy Spirit to come down off the ladder! God didn't do this. We are taught, corrected, inspired, and reproved by the Word of God, not by tragedy.

> *All scripture is given by inspiration of God, and is profitable for doctrine, for reproof, for correction, for instruction in righteousness. 2 Timothy 3:16*

Others believe that God doesn't necessarily ordain evil but He allows it. God showed me that His allowing any kind of evil would be like Him signing a petition to make it happen. Anytime we sign a petition we are saying that we are in agreement with the purpose of the petition. If God allows tragedy, then He is in agreement with it.

What's the difference, then, between ordaining it or allowing it? Either way it has the same outcome. The pain is still there; the loss and grief are still there; people's lives are still changed forever. God would never sign on for tragedy because then He would be in agreement with the destruction. According to Jeremiah 29:11, God is never in agreement with any kind of death or destruction for anyone.

Would you allow your child to cross a highway with cars coming in both directions, knowing he or she would get hit? Of course not. We would do anything we could to protect our children. If we, with our limited capacity, would go to great lengths to protect our children, how much more would God protect His children?

> *If ye then, being evil, know how to give good gifts unto your children, how much more shall your Father which is in heaven give good things to them that ask him? Matthew 7:11*

You may say that the Old Testament is full of God either ordaining or allowing death and destruction. This is true, but we are now in the new covenant—a season of forgiveness, grace, and mercy extended to us because of what Jesus accomplished on the cross. God is no longer angry because Jesus took all of His wrath onto Himself.

He now operates differently with us. Jeremiah 29:11 clearly states that God has a perfect plan for every person's life. But He doesn't force us to fulfill that plan. He has given us a free will to choose either life or death.

I have set before you life and death, blessing and cursing: therefore choose life. Deuteronomy 30:19

It's our choice; we can make right choices or wrong choices, but it's our choice. We control our destinies, not God!

And then there's the devil.

Submit yourselves therefore to God. Resist the devil, and he will flee from you. James 4:7

Some things are from God, and some things are from the devil. But it seems that most of the time the devil gets a free pass. He is not even mentioned when bad things happen, but the truth is that the devil is behind all evil, whether directly or indirectly.

> *The thief cometh not, but for to steal, and to kill, and to destroy. John 10:10*

Words cannot express the sadness our country has felt over the Newtown, Connecticut, school shooting tragedy. Many articles have been written, as well as TV broadcasts made, trying to answer the questions "Why did this happen? Could God have intervened? Does the devil have more power than God?"

The devil does not have more power than God. God has ultimate authority, but He does not directly control what happens on earth. Why? Because He gave us a free will, dominion, and authority over the earth (see Ps. 115:16), and we can use it as we please. If we cooperate with Him, the outcome is good; if not, the outcome is evil.

We have a free will to choose life or death, sickness or health, poverty or prosperity, bondage or deliverance. We have a free will to live God's way or the devil's way. It was never God's intention that man would choose evil. His plan for us is always good, but we have to cooperate with Him. And many, sad to say, don't.

One news commentator had asked, "Why did God give us a free will?" This answer is simple too. God didn't want to force us to love Him. He wanted us to choose on our own to love Him. He wanted us to choose to have a relationship with Him. We are the same way. We would not want to have to force someone to love us; we would want that person to love us of his or her own desire. And that is what God wants as well.

What God has set in place, He will not change. We will always have a free will, and God will never override it. This should help us understand why these things happen.

So, yes, there is a reason for everything, but we must make sure that we understand those reasons correctly. The reason bad things happen is because of sin in the world, unbelief, or the devil. God has nothing to do with evil. Jesus never brought sickness, disease, or any other tragedy onto anyone while He was here. Jesus went about doing good!

How God anointed Jesus of Nazareth with the Holy Ghost and with power: who went about doing good, and healing all that were oppressed of the devil; for God was with him. Acts 10:38

Wherever there is good, there is God: *Every good gift and every perfect gift is from above (James 1:17).* In the book of Job, God was very serious about what was said about Him and about the way He was represented. God spoke to Job's friends, saying, *Ye have not spoken of me the thing that is right (42:7).* We must make sure we represent our Lord correctly, as a good God who has a good and perfect plan for each of our lives. God is love, and where there is love, there is no evil whatsoever! Thank You, Jesus!

Chapter Twenty

You Be the Judge

Judge not, that ye be not judged. For with what judgment ye judge, ye shall be judged: and with what measure ye mete, it shall be measured to you again.

Matthew 7:1-2

Two things are made clear in this scripture: First, we are not to judge; and second, if we do judge, we will be judged and will receive the same amount of judgment that we give out. I believe Jesus was warning us to be careful how we judge.

There is a right kind of judging and a wrong kind of judging. An example would be waiting in a doctor's office. Your appointment was for 2 p.m., but at 2:30 you're still waiting. Making a judgment that the doctor is running late is fine; that's obvious. But to make the judgment that he has no consideration for his patients or that he only cares about making money is the wrong kind of judging.

Those judgments may be true, but Jesus warns us to be careful not to make them. This is the condemnation type of judging Jesus cautions us against. Judging the circumstance for what it is is one thing, but judging the motives of someone's actions is quite another and should be avoided.

Why would Jesus warn us against this kind of judgment? He does so to protect us from receiving the same kind of judgment from others. Rather than looking at God as someone who just wants to be in control by telling us what to do, we should understand that whatever He tells us to do or warns us against is for our own good. God is a good God!

> *And why beholdest thou the mote that is in thy brother's eye, but considerest not the beam that is in thine own eye? Matthew 7:3*

A mote is a tiny piece of something. A beam is a thick piece of wood, metal, or concrete. The universal interpretation of this verse is that we should not judge others for their small sin when we have a bigger sin in our lives. Yet, James 2:10 says *for whosoever shall keep the whole law, and yet offend in one point, he is guilty of all.* To God, sin is sin. The consequences of each sin may vary according to the circumstances, or according to how many people are affected, but to God, there are no levels of sin. I do not interpret this scripture to mean a small sin versus a big sin.

What I do believe is that the mote can be a sin or failing of some kind, even in the area of making a condemning judgment of others, but I believe the beam is much more than that. The beam is the judgment we hold toward the person who committed the sin. If this is true, then judging another's sin is actually worse than the sin itself.

The Message Bible interprets Matthew 7:1-5 this way:

> *Don't pick on people, jump on their failures, criticize their faults—unless, of course, you want the same treatment. That critical spirit has a way of boomeranging. It's easy to see a smudge on your neighbor's face and be oblivious to the ugly sneer on your own. Do you have the nerve to say, 'Let me wash your face for you,' when your own face is distorted by contempt? It's this whole traveling road–show mentality all over again, playing a holier–than–thou part instead of just living your part. Wipe that ugly sneer off your own face, and you might be fit to offer a washcloth to your neighbor.*

Judging is vocalizing *what* the person did and *why* he or she did it. It seems too easy to look down on someone who has done wrong and start judging. The reason we do this is to make us look and feel better about ourselves. We begin to reason that we would never do such a thing, or we are way above that kind of living. We would be wise to remember 1 Corinthians 10:12— *Wherefore let him that thinketh he standeth take heed lest he fall.* No one is totally above getting it all right. That's why there's grace for all of us. Thank God!

So rather than looking down on someone's shortcomings, we should pray for a revelation of God's grace to be poured out so that person can see the goodness of God. God's goodness helps change people's minds about their behavior in the first place. Looking again at Matthew 7:3, the original Greek word for *behold* is *blepo. Blepo* first means "to see." We are able to see what this person is doing or has done; it's plain and clear. There's no question about it. This is the right kind of judging; it's proper discernment.

But the word *blepo* also means "to gaze." Now, our seeing it for what it is, which was okay, turns into gazing. We are now seriously thinking about what this person has done.

The definition of *blepo* also goes further to mean "to contemplate or reflect deeply on a particular subject." Here is where our thoughts become more intense.

Blepo also indicates "weighing carefully and examining." Our mind is now entrenched in what this person did. We are now examining the entire situation as well as the character of that person.

And finally, *blepo* means "to compare." This is the ultimate progression of this word. At the end, we compare this person to ourselves. We begin with properly discerning what this person has done; then we gaze upon it for a while, which leads to us reflecting deeply on the person's behavior, examining it carefully, leading us to making a condemning judgment on the entire situation and character of the person. Then we compare this person to ourselves, commending ourselves, of course, that we would never do such a thing.

Bible teacher Joyce Meyer accurately stated that we see others through a magnifying glass, but we see ourselves through rose-colored glasses. How true!

Matthew 7:4 continues, *Or how wilt thou say to thy brother...* [This implies that we are now going to try to help others with their sin by speaking to them.] ... *Let me pull out the mote out of thine eye; and, behold a beam is in thine own eye? (brackets mine).*

Eye here does not mean a physical eye; it simply means the eyes of the mind or our thinking. This is obvious as we know that where there is sin, there is a need for repentance, which means we need to change our thinking.

This verse is clearly asking how we could possibly help others do away with sin while we are in judgment of them at the same time. The answer is that we can't.

> *Feed the flock of God which is among you, taking the oversight thereof, not by constraint, but willingly; not for filthy lucre, but of a ready mind; Neither as being lords over Gods heritage, but being ensembles to the flock. 1 Peter 5:2-3*

These passages tell us that we are to teach and minister to others, watching over them with care, not because we are forced to but because we sincerely want the best for them. There should be no thought of gaining something for ourselves in the process. We are not to oversee people with force by being demanding, but we should be gentle examples to them. How could anyone minister this way while holding a judgmental attitude toward the person being ministered to?

> *Thou hypocrite, first cast out the beam out of thine own eye; and then shalt thou see clearly to cast out the mote out of thy brother's eye. Matthew 7:5*

How do we do this? How do we cast this judgmental attitude out so we can truly minister to others? Verses 7-8 give us the answer: *Ask, and it shall be given you; seek, and ye shall find; knock, and it shall be opened unto you: For everyone that asketh receiveth; and he that seekers findeth; and to him that knocketh it shall be opened.*

Keeping this verse in its context, I believe it is still talking about being judgmental. We are told to ask, meaning to ask God for what we need, like an answer to why we are judging in the first place. Ask Him about our heart. Ask Him to reveal the real root of the problem. God will show us.

Then we are told to seek, meaning to seek what we don't know about this person we are judging or about the circumstances. God promises if we seek, we will find. Then we are told to knock, and when the door is opened, we finally receive revelation on overcoming judging. The next few verses promise that God will answer our prayers.

Verse 12 seems to be the bookend to verse 1: *Therefore all things whatsoever ye would that men should do to you, do ye even so to them: for this is the law and the prophets.* If you don't want to be judged, then do not judge. Treat others the way you want to be treated. If you don't want people to gossip about you, then don't gossip about others. If, when you fail, you want people to be understanding and compassionate then treat others that way. It's really that simple.

There are two things I try to practice daily: One is to learn how to forgive the one I may be judging. I get in touch with Christ, my Forgiver. Realizing how much I've been forgiven and seeing God's forgiveness toward that person prompts me to truly forgive others.

I also train myself to see others through the eyes of God. His love was so great for them that He died for them.

He is never mad at them. In fact, He is their cheerleader, always encouraging them to move forward in Him. He is long-suffering toward them and looks at them only through His Son, Jesus. He sees them righteous, whole, complete, forgiven, and on and on. He treats them the exact way He treats us! The same mercy He extends to us, He extends to them! So who are we to hold judgment?

Finally, we must be the judge of ourselves.

> *Keep watch over yourselves and all the flock of which the Holy Spirit has made you overseers. Acts 20:28 (NIV)*

We are to keep watch over ourselves *first* and then the flock. We need to check ourselves and rightly judge ourselves first to make sure we are free from the wrong kind of judging. Then we can properly minister to others with great results!

As New Testament believers we are blessed to enjoy this dispensation of mercy and grace. At the cross, all judgment for sin was put onto Jesus; we are no longer being judged for sin. This is all because of God's love for us. Because God no longer judges us for sin, shouldn't we follow

His example by not judging others for their sin? Let's begin to look at others through the eyes of Jesus!

God's Word is filled with treasures that are hidden for us—not from us—and that are worth far more than gold or any other earthly treasure. As we diligently search the scriptures we will learn how to apply the teachings in this book, including how to rely on grace instead of self-effort, how to truly give our cares and worries to Jesus, how to practically use our God-given authority to fight Satan and win, and much more. The ball is in our court. God has already done everything He can to ensure our success in this life through the death and resurrection of His Son, Jesus. Let's not let His promises go to waste. Let's seek them out, find them, and walk in them toward a life of victory!

Prayer to Receive Jesus as Your Lord and Savior

This is where your new life begins. Once you receive His gift of salvation you become brand new with the nature of God residing on the inside of you!

To receive Jesus as your Lord and Savior and to become born again, simply pray the following prayer aloud:

Jesus, I am sorry for my sins. I believe You died for my sins and that God raised You from the dead. I receive Your forgiveness, and I make You the Savior and Lord of my life. Thank You for saving me.

Congratulations! You are now a brand-new creation. Your Spirit man is forever changed: *Therefore if any man be in Christ, he is a new creature: old things are passed away; behold, all things are become new (2 Cor. 5:17).*

Prayer to Receive the Baptism of the Holy Spirit

God's desire is to empower you to live your new life. Jesus Himself was baptized in the Holy Spirit before He ever began His public ministry. If Jesus needed it then we need it as well (see Matt. 3:13-17).

To receive the baptism in the Holy Spirit, pray the following prayer aloud:

> *Lord, I want to be empowered to live this new life. I know this is a gift from You and that I need it to live the abundant life You've promised me. Please fill me now with Your Holy Spirit with the evidence of speaking in tongues. Thank You for baptizing me. By faith, I fully expect to speak in other tongues as You give me the utterance (see Acts 2:4). In Jesus' name, amen.*

Now begin thanking and praising God for baptizing you, and begin speaking the syllables He gives you. This is the language the Holy Spirit has given to you. To speak this language aloud is an act of your will by faith. God will never force you to speak—it will always be your decision. Enjoy your new spiritual language as often as you like, and as you do, you will build yourself up in your faith: *But ye, beloved, building up yourselves on your most holy faith, praying in the Holy Ghost (Jude 1:20).*

If you'd like additional information regarding salvation or the baptism of the Holy Spirit, please see the resources at the end of this book that follow under "Suggested Readings."

Suggested Readings

There are many nuggets of truth that need to be mined out of God's Word in the same way that the woman searched diligently until she found her lost coin (see Luke 15:8-10). I recommend the following books for an in-depth teaching on **WHO** we are in Christ, **WHAT** we have in Christ, and **HOW** to use what we have been given:

Spirit, Soul & Body by Andrew Wommack: The **WHO;** this book provides foundational teaching describing what actually happens when we are born again. It explains how we are made of three parts, one of which is our Spirit man that becomes brand new when we make Jesus our Lord and Savior.

You've Already Got It! (So Quit Trying to Get It) by Andrew Wommack: The **WHAT;** whatever it is we need, we already have! Through this book, you'll learn how everything we could ever need was all provided for by Jesus at the cross. Knowing what we actually have inside our born-again spirit motivates us to change the negative circumstances in our lives.

The Believer's Authority: What You Didn't Learn in Church by Andrew Wommack: The **HOW;** this book will help you learn how to recognize Satan's tactics then how to fight against them in order to win every battle in your life.

The New You and The Holy Spirit by Andrew Wommack: Learn exactly what transpires when you make the decision to follow the Lord and become born again, as well as the benefits you receive through the baptism in the Holy Spirit.

You can order these books and more at: www.awmi.net.

God's Best Is for You Too! by Al and Angie Buhrke: Al and Angie share their personal stories of trials and triumph. This book is an encouragement to those facing trials in their lives by showing how staying single-minded on the Word of God produces positive results.

You can order this book by email: victory life.aa@gmail.com.